Harnessing the Power of Resistance

A Guide for Educators

Jared Scherz

EYE ON EDUCATION
6 DEPOT WAY WEST, SUITE 106
LARCHMONT, NY 10538
(914) 833–0551
(914) 833–0761 fax
www.eyeoneducation.com

Library of Congress Cataloging-in-Publication Data

Scherz, Jared.
　　Harnessing the power of resistance : a guide for educators / Jared Scherz.
　　　　p. cm.
　　Includes bibliographical references.
　　ISBN 1-930556-76-4
　　1. School management and organization. 2. School personnel management. 3. Teacher-student relationships. 4. Teacher-principal relationships. 5. Interpersonal confrontation. I. Title.

LB2806.S3414 2004
371.2--dc22

　　　　　　　　　　　　　　　　　　　　　　2004043200

10 9 8 7 6 5 4 3 2

Editorial and production services provided by
Richard H. Adin Freelance Editorial Services
52 Oakwood Blvd., Poughkeepsie, NY 12603-4112
(914-471-3566)

Also Available from EYE ON EDUCATION

What Great Principals Do *Differently*:
15 Things That Matter Most
Todd Whitaker

Dealing with Difficult Teachers, Second Edition
Todd Whitaker

Dealing with Difficult Parents
(And with Parents in Difficult Situations)
Todd Whitaker and Douglas Fiore

Motivating & Inspiring Teachers
The Educational Leader's Guide for Building Staff Morale
Todd Whitaker, Beth Whitaker, and Dale Lumpa

What Great Teachers Do *Differently*:
14 Things That Matter Most
Todd Whitaker

Supervision Across the Content Areas
Sally J. Zepeda and R. Stewart Mayers

The Principal as Instructional Leader:
A Handbook for Supervisors
Sally J. Zepeda

Instructional Leadership for School Improvement
Sally J. Zepeda

Standards of Practice for Teachers
A Brief Handbook
P. Diane Frey, Mary Jane Smart, and Sue A. Walker

Achievement Now!
How To Assure No Child is Left Behind
Dr. Donald J. Fielder

Bravo Principal!
Building Relationships with Actions That Value Others
Sandra Harris

The ISLLC Standards in Action:
Principal's Handbook
Carol Engler

Teaching Matters:
Motivating & Inspiring Yourself
Todd and Beth Whitaker

101 Answers for New Teachers and Their Mentors:
Effective Teaching Tips for Daily Classroom Use
Annette L. Breaux

Data Analysis for Continuous School Improvement
Victoria L. Bernhardt

School Leader Internship: Developing, Monitoring,
and Evaluating Your Leadership Experience
Gary Martin, William Wright, and Arnold Danzig

Handbook on Teacher Evaluation:
Assessing and Improving Performance
James Stronge & Pamela Tucker

Handbook on Educational Specialist Evaluation:
Assessing & Improving Performance
James Stronge & Pamela Tucker

Handbook on Teacher Portfolios
for Evaluation and Professional Development
Pamela Tucker & James Stronge

The Confrontational Parent:
A Practical Guide for School Leaders
Dr. Charles M. Jaksec III

Beyond Measure:
Neglected Elements of Accountability in Schools
Edited by Patricia E. Holland

About the Author

Jared Scherz is the founder of Integrative Training and Consulting (ITC), a multifaceted organization designed to help schools succeed. ITC focuses on school improvement at the systems level and the individual level. An executive coach with over ten years of experience consulting with school personnel, Jared is a pioneer in the area of educational transformation.

Before ITC, Jared directed several social service agencies and worked privately as a therapist/coach for managers and other professionals.

Jared earned his bachelor's degree at SUNY Binghamton, his master's degree in education at Penn State University, and will earn his doctorate in clinical psychology at Saybrook University. His dissertation addressed school violence prevention.

Jared has worked as a school counselor and consultant in various urban and rural schools. From the rural mountains of Pennsylvania to the urban neighborhoods of inner city Chicago, he has experienced a wide range of problems, including gangs and domestic violence.

On February 29, 2000, a first grader in Flint, Michigan, shot and killed a classmate. This tragic event brought home to Jared the tremendous need for whole-school improvement. He disagreed with the "experts" who came on television to discuss the need for increased prevention efforts. It wasn't their proactive stance that concerned him, but their narrow vision of how to reduce potential student aggression. What seemed to be missing was an appreciation for the school culture—the organizational setting that influences relationships among students and faculty that ultimately sets the school's course toward conflict and peer aggression or toward student learning and school success.

Acknowledgments

I would like to thank several people for their input; without their help this book would not have been completed. To Nathan, Jane, Eileen, and Nancy for their creative genius. To Barb for all her shared experiences and experiments. To the Gestalt Institute of Cleveland who refined the theory and practice outlined throughout this book. To Celia Bohannon for turning my words into fluid and cohesive sentences. To my wife and father for their patience and feedback. And to Bob Sickles, for believing in me.

This book is dedicated to my godchildren TJ & Ryan, the young people in my family: Carla, Joaquin, Laurel, Joel, Melissa, Breanna, Samantha, Ilana, Nicole, and to my child Cassie. Hoping to help make our educational system a better place for them and others.

Table of Contents

Part I

Developing a Plan

1
Goals for Reading this Book

In many ways, working in schools resembles sailing a boat. To harness the power of the wind, sailors continually adjust the angle of the tiller and trim of the sail. They learn to respect the forces of nature—the wind, the water, the shoals along the shore. Working with these forces leads to smooth sailing. Experienced sailors know that moving with the wind takes less energy than moving against it. But that doesn't always mean going with the flow; for instance, the boat must meet the waves head on or risk capsizing. Finally, the master sailor appreciates making the journey as much as reaching the destination.

Some schools face a turbulent voyage, with wave after wave of challenges and little opportunity for rest. Educators in these schools may feel as though they are drowning in problems—problems that seem to run alongside, keeping up with them no matter how quickly they move. Somehow, these schools manage to stay afloat. They survive because the educators who steer their course know the importance of their work, have the fortitude to endure, and—most importantly—learn to work with the resources at hand.

But like master sailors, true educators seek more than survival. I hope that this book will help educators find enjoyment, even fulfillment, in their work.

I want educators to wake up each morning excited about going to work. I want them to experience their full potential for growth in a this essential job. I want them to go home at the end of the day not drained of their energy, sapped of their strength, but with a sense of accomplishment.

How will this book help? I believe that educators who fully understand the nature of resistance, who know how to use resistance to their benefit, can do more than survive. They can harness the energy of the workplace. They can reach their chosen destination—and find satisfaction in the voyage.

I hope that this book will help you improve your relationships with colleagues, with students, and with others in the administrative hierarchy of schools. I hope that you will learn more about the ways you interact with the forces that shape your journey, and that you will gain confidence through this personal discovery.

Improve Your Relationships with Colleagues

Cliques can develop in any organization; people naturally gravitate to others with similar interests and shared experiences. Schools, in particular, often see cliques that can split the faculty. On the other hand, professional relationships or even friendships can form between people who seem less likely to connect—and here too, schools can offer a greater potential for deeper and more meaningful relationships.

Why do schools have this advantage over other social services and for-profit industries? First of all, in a small to mid-sized school community, people may get to know each other in ways that don't happen in larger companies. Secondly, the job of teaching can evoke strong emotions—passion, frustration, pride—because educators see how their efforts directly affect the lives of others. Professionals in industry may lack this sense of immediate connection with the "product." Thirdly, educators can experience the comradeship of working in the trenches: Scarce resources, inadequate financial compensation, and other forms of adversity may cause frustration, but they can also foster a team mentality among those who meet these obstacles together.

This book presents resistance as a force inherent in all relationships. It offers you the opportunity to learn to appreciate and value resistance. As you read this book, think of colleagues you feel close to, and envision how they can be brought closer; consider those you feel distant from, and think of ways to make them your loyal allies. Try out some of the ideas outlined here in your relationship with the colleague who challenges you most. The results may surprise you.

Engage Students
with Greater Ease

In this era of cell phones and video games and DVDs, of fast-paced technology, and immediate gratification, educators must work hard to keep their students' attention. Students today often face limits and consequences with a new audacity and view grades with a strong sense of entitlement. When independent activities such as homework make students feel isolated, they resist. When classroom exercises interfere with their need for belonging and social affirmation, they resist. Even veteran teachers often wonder how to respond to this resistance.

This book offers suggestions for appreciating how and why students resist learning. It proposes ways for educators to meet students' needs in a safe and nurturing environment. The book introduces teachers to the power of connecting with students—a task that requires creativity and a willingness to go beyond the expected. It doesn't necessarily mean adding work but altering the quality of existing work.

As you read this book, think of students who act out their frustrations in your school, in your classroom. Focus on the ones with whom you feel least connected. Throughout this book you will be asked to begin to understand their resistance to you and your resistance to them, and to establish the bonds you may currently view as unlikely.

Decrease Tensions
Within the Hierarchy of School

Picture the complex web of relationships that makes up the hierarchy of your school. Identify the hot spots—the links that create tension rather than provide support. How would transforming such relationships change the way you feel about going to work each day?

Teachers who enjoy supportive relationships with administrators find it easier to acquire the resources they need for effective instruction, gain support in dealing with difficult students, and elicit feedback leading to professional growth. Administrators who build supportive relationships with teachers find it easier to launch new programs, raise morale, retain good teachers, and sustain a productive learning community.

Who has the power to transform relationships within the school hierarchy? Often, teachers view this as a job for administrators. They fail to recognize the ways their own behavior supports or inhibits healthy relationships. This book seeks to change that perception.

As you read this book, think of how people in your school respond to authority, power, and control. Consider how you might work with this resistance, rather than struggling against it. Pick the hot spot that bothers you the most, and explore ways to deal with it—not just to endure it, but to transform it.

Improve Your Confidence Through Self-Awareness

What enables one sailor to face a storm at sea with confidence, while another trembles? The intrepid sailor relies on experience, solid skills, a seaworthy craft—even a precise awareness of the boat's limitations and vulnerabilities. In all walks of life, self-confidence rests on self-awareness.

Self-aware people take ownership of their lives. They blame others less and hold themselves more accountable. As a result, they tend to form relationships more readily and maintain them more successfully. People who acknowledge their own limitations can work more effectively to overcome them; people who recognize their own needs can take steps toward having those needs met.

In particular, self-aware people learn to identify the forces that push them toward sameness and pull them toward change—the tension perceived as resistance. As you read, I hope you will develop a better appreciation for the dynamics of resistance in your own life and greater confidence in your ability to deal with the resistance of others as well.

Happy sailing!

Part II

Appreciating Resistance

2

Understanding Resistance

Typical Definitions of Resistance

Dictionaries define *resistance* as *confrontation* or *opposition*. Synonyms include *battle, struggle, fight*—terms that denote conflict. The term has an inherently negative connotation. Interestingly enough, the dictionaries list *surrender* as the antonym, conjuring up images of victory and defeat. In this view, people who put up resistance threaten those who hold power. The verbs describing the anticipated response include *breakdown, overcome, overpower, crush, wear down*—at best, *forestall* or *avoid*.

Imagine a marriage in which this mind-set holds sway. A difference of opinion arises; the partners cannot reach agreement. Some form of battle ensues. One partner emerges victorious, the other wounded by defeat. Depending on the tactics the winner has employed, the loser may feel overpowered, manipulated, or disregarded.

What happens if this continues over any sustained period of time? Win-lose outcomes create distance between the two sides, leading to a loss of intimacy. When one partner holds more power than the other, communications suffer. Covert maneuvers replace a more open and honest mode of interaction.

Meanwhile, the two individuals develop different habits of relating to others. The person who usually comes out on top learns to prefer this outcome in other situations as well. "Winners" tend to seek out people they can overpower; yet they submit to those with more authority. They live within a system of hierarchical patterns, where survival of the fittest is the rule. Without the vulnerability and receptivity of genuine relationships, they often encounter loneliness.

The partner who more often loses the battle experiences the situation quite differently. Feelings of helplessness, anxiety, and depression cloud the horizon. Habitual "losers" may come to believe that what they do no longer matters; nothing brings success. This victim mentality can also lead to feelings of hopelessness and a sense of isolation.

We can observe similar patterns of behavior in institutional settings, and especially in school systems, which traditionally follow a hierarchical design. Leaders—school superintendents, principals, and even classroom teachers—often assume that the authority of their position will induce others to follow their directives. Unfortunately, however, this can cause problems. True, their subordinates may do as they are told much of the time—but often a hidden backlash occurs.

A classroom teacher who rules with an iron fist engenders compliance, but also fear. Students hesitate to challenge the established order because they do not want to sustain emotional harm. Instead, they learn to carve out their own territory of safety within the classroom—a larger territory for the most powerful, a small space for the weakest. This pecking order creates fragmentation; the class never sees itself as a cohesive whole. As individuals band together to gain strength, cliques form. In recent times, students have even begun to challenge this authority outright, setting up constant power struggles in the classroom.

Among faculty, the process becomes slightly more complex and often subtler. Veteran teachers typically hold the greatest power. Others seek to align themselves with the veterans to gain strength. When the resulting coalition supports values that differ from those of the institutional leaders, a power struggle ensues. Each side seeks to retain as much control as possible without resorting to outright hostility. Tactics may alternate between direct opposition and more passive or covert foot-dragging. The constant skirmishing leads to a fragmented system, with stubborn factions defending and promoting their divergent views about the right way to run the school. An atmosphere of discontent, distrust, and inflexibility pervades the school culture. Such a school will find it difficult to adapt to the constantly changing demands that buffet it from within and without.

Even if such outright factions do not materialize, various forms of passive aggression can take their toll. The school leadership and the faculty may refrain from outright power struggles, but if they also refuse to explore and understand their differences, they will remain at odds. You will find examples of these less obvious scenarios throughout this book.

The Balance Perspective

Another school of thought—within the field of gestalt theory—views resistance **not** as a hostile force but as an ever-present state, a natural condition that creates the necessary tension for change. Without resistance, change would occur either too rapidly or not at all.

Sit upright for a moment. What keeps your head from nodding forward? The muscles of your shoulder and neck resist relaxation. Even without your conscious attention, resistance holds your head erect. On the other hand, though your eyelids may droop with fatigue, you can resist falling asleep. On this very physical level (within your body), resistance governs the pace of change.

In another intrapersonal example, you may feel dissatisfaction with something or somebody in your life—perhaps a job or a relationship. Should you intervene in some way? Wait it out, or make a change? The forces that tug you one way or another at various levels—physiological, emotional, cognitive—create uncertainty in your life. This constant state of tension, or resistance, actually helps mobilize you to take action to meet your needs.

How does this work? Each of us, consciously and unconsciously, seeks to maintain an optimal level of tension in our lives. If the tension is too low, we become flat and unresponsive. If the tension is too high, we experience stress that exhausts us mentally and physically. In a delicate balancing act, we try to keep the tension at optimal level.

Think of a fisherman letting out line. Too much slack allows the fish to take the bait and escape before the fisherman can respond. Too taut a line warns the fish that something is amiss. The successful fisherman works to keep the tension just right.

For the most part, we cannot sustain concentration on maintaining the 'right' balance of tension. We face numerous choices and conflicts in the course of a day that many of our decisions occur beneath the level of our awareness. If we focus on the end result we pay little heed to how we get there. Like someone flying on autopilot, we do not recognize the level of uncertainty in our lives. When we do acknowledge uncertainty, we may feel out of control—so instead we pretend not to notice. We behave as if we have it all together. Disregarding any ambivalence we may experience, we choose one direction and head there, indiscriminately.

We could take a different approach—an approach that views ambivalence as normal, potentially useful, and often valuable. We could acknowledge that change creates uncertainty—and ambivalence, or resistance—in individuals and in organizations. We could become curious about this ambivalence, explore it at a deeper level, and perhaps better understand its nature. As we experience resistance with curiosity, we may discover its protective, curative, and creative aspects. We may find ways to harness its energy to better meet our needs.

Those who view resistance as a threat may find it hard to take this approach. If you fall into this category, you might try a little experiment. You don't have to apply this approach immediately in your everyday life—but do pay attention to your own experience of resistance as you read this book. When a concept falls outside your understanding, recognize this lack of fit and watch what you do with it. Do you dismiss the idea as silly or stupid? Do you gloss over the suggestion as if you had not read it? Do you pretend to understand the concept, even if you can't make heads or tails of it? Do you place your own interpretation on it, even when you are confident it is not what's intended? Where does your response take you?

Notice how the simple act of curiously examining your own reactions increases your self-awareness. Look for signs that greater self-awareness increases your tolerance for ambiguity. Perhaps, as you learn more about your reactions, biases, projections, and values, you will begin to look forward to self-discovery. Perhaps you will come to view resistance as energizing, creative, and important for regulating the systems within your body, within your classroom, within your school. Perhaps you will decide to harness that energy. If so, you will get more from this book than you thought possible.

It All Begins with Curiosity

I once felt frustrated when staff members arrived late at "my" meetings. I didn't know or care why they came late; I just objected to what I saw as a lack of respect. But as I explored my experience further, I found myself wondering whether the meetings actually had significant value. Perhaps my staff felt the same way. If they didn't find the meetings useful or meaningful, why should they arrive promptly? This realization opened the door to a new approach. Perhaps including staff members in setting the agenda would increase their investment in the meeting—and get them there on time. Granted, such an exploration takes work, but in this instance it helped me to become a better leader.

Let's look at another example. A teacher nearing retirement came to me for coaching. She described her problem as procrastination: Her retirement paperwork lay unfinished on her kitchen table. She insisted that she needed to fill out the paperwork before summer vacation; otherwise, she worried, bureaucratic red tape might delay her departure. She had tried strategy after strategy to get the job done, but nothing seemed to work. She asked me to help.

I suggested that we explore the possibility of resistance. Even though she very much wanted to end her career as a teacher, perhaps strong forces resisted this move. "Ridiculous!" she responded. After 30 years in the classroom, she did not want to continue another day. I asked her to humor me just for a moment and describe what her retirement might bring. She paused. Tears came to her eyes; she began to sob. It seemed that despite her strong intention to end her career, she worried about her identity, her sense of accomplishment, and (most importantly) her own mortality. Beginning her retirement meant nearing her own death.

Had I focused on concrete strategies for tackling piles of paperwork, we probably would have accomplished little. Instead, my prompting led her to recognize the forces for and against change, allowing her to more fully experience her resistance to ending her career. As she gained a deeper awareness of her fears, she came to understand her lack of follow-through.

Like individuals, organizations benefit from paying attention to the realities of the present before seeking the outcomes of change. An organization must slow down to gain insight into what it is, what it does, how it meets its goals, and other defining questions. The core of this exploration lies in determining the forces for and against a potential change.

As an institution (in our case, a school) builds awareness of these forces, fragmentation gives way to greater cohesion. Both sides—the forces for sameness and the forces for change—come to appreciate the very polarity of their views. For instance, a person who favors structure and direction will balance another who supports autonomy and freedom. A group that seeks to implement a stricter response to student violence will gain balance from a group that attaches importance to remediation. When the separate individuals or groups representing these opposing forces appreciate the importance of this balance, they can become allies rather than adversaries. When each recognizes the other's needs, they can work together to find a solution satisfactory to both.

It may help to remember that each person or group—no matter how committed to one side—also experiences, to some degree, the contrary force. For example, a teacher who openly voices her dislike of classroom observations will also harbor curiosity about her observer's opinions. (Keep in mind, too, that those who direct all their energy toward one outcome may not recognize this polarity in themselves.)

The Power of Resistance

Organizations constantly experience internal and external pressure—pressure to maintain sameness, pressure to achieve change. This persistent pressure causes stress; the greater the pressure, the greater the stress. While the school building itself may not show cracks, the people within feel the effects.

The force we call resistance represents a way to manage this pressure, to strike a balance between flux and stagnation. As a force of nature, resistance maintains the ecosystems of our planet. The seashore resists the ocean's waves; the waves break down the sand on the shore. The population of one species swells until a predator species checks its growth. The interplay between these forces leads to balance. It is this interplay—this competition, this friction—that we experience as resistance. And if we accept resistance as natural and inevitable, we can work with it. When we don't, we may be overwhelmed by its power.

The Cycle of Experience

"I'm feeling hungry, but it's not lunchtime yet." "I wish I could ask her to lunch, but I'm afraid she'll say no." "I want to be home playing in my garden, but I'm stuck here at work." We may experience these conflicting needs or wants only as "background noise"—sensations we ignore as we focus on grading papers, meeting with parents, or filling out budget requests. If we pay attention, we can take action to meet these needs. The cycle in which we become aware of our needs, respond, and move on is referred to as the *cycle of experience*.

Let's look first at the individual or intrapersonal cycle of experience. The process begins, for example, when you notice a physical sensation—fatigue, lightheadedness, a rumbling stomach. You pay attention long enough to identify the unmet need: hunger. Mobilizing energy, you respond; you grab a banana, fix a sandwich, chug a milkshake. The sensations that alerted you begin to dissipate. You move on.

What if something blocks or interrupts the process? You're stuck in a meeting; you're on a diet and trying to restrict food intake; you have to finish that pesky report by three o'clock.

The energy you would have mobilized to satisfy your need must find another outlet. The blocked energy creates the experience of tension, perhaps in the form of headaches or fatigue.

Similar processes and effects characterize the external or interpersonal cycle of experience. For example, perhaps classroom teachers object when the school counselor takes students out of class for counseling sessions. If teachers were to meet with the counselor, each may gain a greater appreciation for the other's intent. Understanding gives way to a search for common ground; after all both sides want what is best for the child even if they intervene at different levels. They are then able to work out a system to schedule appointments that take into account both learning and emotional needs. They move on.

But at this level as well, conflicts or differing agendas can block the cycle. Unmet needs create tension. This can lead to communication breakdowns, alignment into factions, and sometimes power struggles. These consequences affect both the school's working environment and the students' learning environment.

At both levels, interruptions to the cycle of experience can limit your awareness of self and others. If you don't pay attention to your sensations of hunger, you avoid contact with yourself. If you recognize your hunger but don't eat, you may be less sensitive to those around you. If you immerse yourself in planning a holiday assembly, you may neglect your contribution to projects that others find more important.

The school setting offers abundant opportunities for feedback about unmet needs, although it may not always be direct and easy to spot. Try paying attention when conflicts arise, or when your agenda differs from that of others. Notice how you respond to a lack of support for your views, or how easily you tolerate differing perspectives. If you or someone you know has difficulty in this area—feeling rejected, discounted, or continuously misunderstood—then perhaps it's time to pay more attention to the signals along the way. If you catch the signals from your body before they become full blown symptoms, the stress of major life disruptions may be circumvented.

How often do we use the word *stress* to describe our experience in schools? Actually, greater awareness might lead us to a better understanding of the tug of opposing forces in our lives. If we stop trying to overcome resistance—if we accept it and explore it—we may learn how to harness its energy.

Summary

- Understanding the nature of resistance means being curious about it, exploring its meaning.
- Those who view resistance as opposition or defiance strengthen its force.
- The balance perspective accepts the constant interplay of forces that maintain sameness and forces that promote change.
- Resistance constantly occurs at the intrapersonal level, the interpersonal level, and the organizational level. Awareness of its effects at each of these levels supports our ability to make informed decisions.
- Individuals and organizations function in a cycle of experience that takes them from unmet needs to satisfaction of those needs.

Suggested Reading

Carter, J. D. (1999). *Becoming a better intervener.* Unpublished manual.

3

Causes
of Resistance

In Chapter 1, we alluded to resistance as a reaction to a perceived or real threat to sameness. We each strive for equilibrium in our lives. Like a gymnast hanging from the apparatus called the rings, we exert our force trying to keep as steady as possible. This conserves our energy for the tasks we face.

When we experience a person or event as potentially disruptive to our balance, we try to minimize the disruption. Standing on the deck of a sailboat, we widen our stance to steady ourselves; striding into a stiff wind, we cross our arms across our chest for protection; wading into the ocean, we brace ourselves against the waves. Emotionally, we make similar responses—sometimes in proportion to the forces that buffet us, sometimes not. Our disproportionate reactions often arise from a simple lack of awareness.

The less attention we pay to the ways we seek balance, the less control we have over this process. The less we recognize our need for safety, the less control we have over feeling safe. When we perceive change as a risk, we work hard to defend against it by controlling ourselves and our environment—a nearly impossible task that often results in frustration and tension.

The physical experience of this tension is multifaceted—tightened muscles, quickened heartbeats, shallow and rapid breathing, body temperature changes, perspiration, swirling thoughts. The mind interprets these bodily changes as either excitement or worry. If the tension continues, increasing amounts of energy become trapped within the body. We may expend our energy on anxiety rather than on action to meet our needs. If this pattern goes on long enough, we sputter to a halt like a car that has run out of fuel.

Organizations can go through a similar process as they attempt to implement change. Rather than moving fluidly from the inception of an idea to its fruition, they encounter traffic jams, roadblocks, and unexpected detours. The journey takes longer than expected; the engine overheats; the driver and the passengers waste time and energy looking for rest stops and repair shops.

What can we do to keep the organization on a steady forward course? How can we implement change in the face of resistance? Perhaps surprisingly, we might shift our sights from our destination to the here and now. We might slow down and take a good look at the road that lies before us.

Resistance is not a static entity with one simple explanation. Rather, it is a process with different underlying reasons, each with its own implications. Until we understand the nature of the resistance we face, we cannot set out to deal with it in a healthy way.

In this chapter, we will explore some common sources of resistance. As you read the examples given here, you will surely think of others from your own experience. Let the examples spark your own thoughts on why people resist change, especially in the school setting—and let those thoughts anchor your ideas about how to manage resistance effectively.

A Desire Not to Give up Something of Value

One middle school had scheduled a common recess for all grades for at least fifteen years. After a new principal took office, she announced a number of changes—among them, staggered recess periods. When asked why, she maintained that older children had been bullying younger children. She blamed a lack of supervision for this problem.

Veteran teachers protested this change among themselves; some even voiced their displeasure to the principal. While they sympathized with the need to prevent bullying, they also didn't want to be blamed for this problem. Their chief objection, however, was that the new schedule would deprive them of time together as a group—informal meeting time that helped them get through the day.

As the teachers demonstrated their resistance, some silently and others more directly, the principal dug in her heels. She perceived their resistance as not caring about the problem; she felt her authority challenged. After hearing what she considered shortsighted and selfish arguments, she implemented her plan almost immediately. Ironically, it turned out that while bullying decreased during recess, it escalated in the hallways and during after-school hours.

What had the principal missed? At first, as she addressed the problem of bullying, she may not have thought about the importance of recess in the teachers' day. When they protested, she simply overruled their objections. Had she explored their resistance, she might have discovered why the teachers valued the all-school recess. They used this time not only to socialize, but as an informal opportunity to exchange knowledge and creative ideas. They could share stories, laugh about them, get support, and relieve stress before it ruined their day. New teachers, in particular, benefitted from the experience of veterans—a high priority of teachers in satisfaction surveys (MetLife Foundation, 2000).

Unfortunately, the teachers in this situation also reacted defensively, expressing their dismay without clearly articulating their concerns in a way that would be received by their administrator. In situations like this, both sides must take responsibility for exploring their own experience, communicating their needs, and paying attention to how their statements are received.

Of important note in this example is that veteran teachers, in particular, often see themselves as the guardians of tradition. While principals, superintendents, and board members come and go, veteran teachers remember a wealth of experience often unknown to others. They can protect and sustain the institution's core values and beliefs, both explicit and implicit, that may otherwise fall by the wayside. When newcomers, especially administrators, present a force for change, veteran teachers typically rise to defend the status quo.

A Misunderstanding
of the Change and its Implications

An urban school district in Chicago decided that home-work needed to have more priority. The school board claimed that teachers placed too little value on homework; the superintendent thought the problem had more to do with parents not holding their children accountable. As the basis for an action plan, he suggested surveying the teachers—fully expecting the results to corroborate his view.

His plan backfired. The teachers interpreted the survey as an accusation that they were not doing their jobs properly. They resented the interruption to their already demanding schedule, but they also suspected that they were being blamed for an issue outside of their control. Many did not fill out the survey; those who did respond answered the questions defiantly, confirming the school board's judgment of their attitude about homework.

The superintendent not only lost the battle with the school board, but also damaged his relationship with the teachers. He announced stricter policies on assigning and collecting homework, but the teachers largely ignored them, and by year's end the new policies faded from the scene.

The people responsible for initiating or implementing a change, of course, have an image of what they intend to achieve. But unless they explain this clearly, others will form their own images—often clouded by their own assumptions, and perhaps even by uncertainty or fear.

How often have you heard someone attribute a new educational policy to budgetary concerns or political considerations? That certainly happened when a major restructuring of the New York City school system in 2003 called for the reorganization of special education programs. How many of the people who resisted these changes might have changed their views if they clearly understood the vision and goals that lay behind them?

A Belief That the Change
Does Not Make Sense for the Organization

An urban high school established a partnership with a local company. Company employees agreed to volunteer a number of hours per week helping students with their homework. As part of the deal, the company provided book bags emblazoned with its logo, one for each teacher and student. Though company officials did not demand that people use these book bags, they did imply that they would appreciate that gesture. Some teachers reacted strongly, refusing to participate in the project because they objected to the company's marketing tactics.

Although this partnership potentially offered financial resources as well as student mentoring, some teachers saw the agreement as "selling out." They did not want to send a message to the students or the community that money equals power and creates obligation. Furthermore, teachers were concerned that the company would begin to impose new requirements on the school, compromising its decision-making autonomy. As it turned out, the company became both embarrassed and offended by the teachers' reaction and rescinded its offer to help.

Teachers care about their schools. They bear the ultimate responsibility for the learning that takes place in their classrooms, and they look carefully at any organizational change that will impact the learning environment. If they view it as a threat to that environment, they will resist—and those initiating the change would do well to take their resistance seriously.

The stakes are high. Overall, the percentage of teachers leaving a school (or leaving the profession) after one year is higher than the national average for all professions. As many as 30 percent quit within the first five years (McAdoo, 2002). Furthermore, the nationwide shortage of qualified teachers increases the opportunity for dissatisfied teachers to move to another school—and they know it. In a recent survey, 21 percent of teachers said they changed schools to improve their working conditions, while 10 percent cited dissatisfaction with the administration. By way of comparison, 25 percent changed schools because of relocation and 24 percent moved for economic reasons (MetLife Foundation, 2000).

Prudent school administrators do everything in their power to ensure that their teachers feel good about the direction their school is taking. When teachers tell them an anticipated change doesn't make sense, they listen.

A Belief That the Change Does Not Make Sense for Themselves

A rural school in Montana recently assigned its faculty the task of creating and maintaining a peer mediation program. Because of recent violence within the district, the decision to implement this program did not come as a complete surprise. The teachers did not object to the program itself, and they knew they would receive the training they needed. However, they worried that another responsibility would overwhelm their already full schedules.

Even people who understand the reasons for change may still have concerns about its implementation and outcome. When school leaders impose new programs, faculty may—quite naturally—think first about how it will affect them. Does the change benefit them directly? Does it add to their workload? Will they be relieved of other tasks to compensate? Even if the workload is adjusted, will the change impose the psychological burden of added responsibility?

Even those who understand and support a change may experience a certain amount of resistance to it; self-preservation is a powerful instinct. In addition, teachers caught between a desire to comply with directives and a need to protect their own interests may feel resentment at the conflict imposed on them.

The leaders who develop new policies may not anticipate this response, particularly if the additional work or responsibility seems simple or routine. It's entirely reasonable for school leaders to assess proposals primarily from the viewpoint of their effect on students. But before announcing changes or issuing directives, they may encounter less resistance if they look at the change from the perspective of the people who must carry them out. Examining this change is only sufficient if those who must implement the change feel as though their experience has been considered.

A Low Tolerance for Change

A 54-year-old teacher distressed by professional and personal problems contacted me for coaching. When I asked why she decided to seek help at this time, she described the incident that put her over the edge. Her administration had changed the school policy regarding time off. For vacation time, teachers were expected to give 48 hours notice (up from 24 hours). Also, teachers requesting sick days were expected to find their own substitutes to cover classes. While not happy about the new policies, she did not have a strong reaction until she learned that a colleague had received permission to take time off with less than 48-hours notice. At that point, she stormed into her principal's office and demanded the same right.

With some embarrassment, she described how she "blew up" at her principal, calling the exception grossly unfair and biased but at the same time insisting that she deserved the same flexibility.

She paused, then told me that a recent separation from her husband had brought dramatic changes in her life. She had to learn about managing her finances, find a new place to live, and deal with the overwhelming loss of her 24 year marriage. Furthermore, I knew she considered herself an ideal employee; in 29 years at this school, she worked well with her colleagues and faithfully followed all directives. However, as a perfectionist she has a hard time adjusting to change.

Fortunately, her principal listened to her feelings about being treated unfairly—and listened long enough to understand why a simple policy change caused her such distress. Instead of engaging in a power struggle about policies and procedures, or minimizing her concerns, he explored the issues underlying her resistance. He learned that she would need to take time off with short notice, because of court obligations and other unexpected requirements.

The teacher told me how much she appreciated his response. Had he taken a hard line, she might have blurted out words she would later regret. Instead, recognizing her outburst as out of character, he provided a safety zone in which she could share openly about her needs.

It isn't always that easy to work with resistance, especially when it seems rooted in a selfish refusal to change. And not every protester is a cooperative teacher acting out of character; some faculty or students seem to spring up with loud objections whenever change occurs. The fact is that some people find even a moderate change threatening. Change heightens their awareness of insecurity; they fear that the resulting stimulation will overwhelm them, and even that they may break down. They resist change in an effort to protect their stability, creating greater instability.

Summary

- Resistance arises for a variety of reasons. Understanding the underlying reason can help prevent power struggles.
- People resist change when they think it will mean losing something they value.
- Sometimes people misinterpret the nature of an intended change or react to the way the change is made.
- Veteran teachers often resist any change that they think would threaten the school's integrity or traditional values.
- People may resist change that adds to their own workload or responsibilities, especially if they do not feel supported or understood.
- Some people, whether by personality or through experience, fear change as a threat to their stability.

Suggested Reading

McAdoo, M. (2002, February). Just passing through: A look at teacher retention. *New York Teacher, City Edition*.

MetLife Foundation. (2001). *Key elements of quality schools* (Issue Brief No. 16). New York: Author.

4

Styles
of Expressing
Resistance

Each of us develops patterns of behavior to manage our own feelings and our interactions with other people. Faced with powerful emotions—anger, jealousy, sadness, joy—we look for ways to keep our balance. If our feelings seem to threaten our stability, we may deny, disown, or disguise them. We may have learned these responses as children, told that "Men don't cry," or "It's not polite for girls to be angry." We may have settled on ways of handling conflict that we are not even aware of.

In this chapter, we will explore six typical patterns of behavior, or personality styles. Each represents one way of responding to change and to challenges, to confrontation and to conflict. Each has both useful and harmful attributes. The examples given here illustrate each personality style in action, though of course most people employ a variety of styles in different situations.

As you read, pay attention to the styles that resonate with you. Think of how you might react in a similar situation. Do your responses match any of these? Think of people you get along well with. Do their styles mesh with yours? Think of people who rub you the wrong way. Do you recognize behaviors in them that you dislike in yourself? Or do they have a completely different style that you find uncomfortable? Does your spouse or significant other have a style similar to yours, or a different style? How about the teacher (or student) you have the most difficulty with?

The answers to these questions may reveal common threads that run through your professional, social, and familial relationships. In particular, what you learn about these personality styles may help you understand how people experience change and how they express their resistance to change.

The Swallower

Susan's principal announces a new initiative to "teach from the side" rather than "lead from the front." The shift in philosophy requires that teachers use more props to spark discussions among the students. (Once a discussion is underway, the teacher is supposed to facilitate the discussion, not manage it.) Teachers can use whatever props they like, but they must find them on their own.

The announcement comes with little warning and no opportunity for discussion. Susan recognizes the change as yet another in a long list of improvement efforts. She also knows that by year's end another initiative will replace it—leaving her with boxes full of props she has purchased at her own considerable expense.

Nevertheless, Susan goes right to work purchasing new items for her classroom and rewriting her lesson plans. She doesn't question the reasoning behind the decision; she doesn't express any irritation at how the principal announced the change. She doesn't even examine her own reaction (or lack of reaction). She just goes along.

In a sense, Susan's response is like eating without chewing—swallowing food whole. People who swallow change without paying attention to its effects on them are asking for emotional indigestion. They can ignore their reactions for a time, but not forever. Sooner or later, they will overload their systems. Stomachaches, headaches, ulcers, even depression can ensue.

The swallower suffers in silence. Others often don't notice how stress takes its toll; swallowers don't impose their problems on coworkers or supervisors. They take direction well; they don't make waves. But when the system reaches overload, swallowers (especially children) often resort to dramatic measures to express their unmet needs.

On the other hand, this style has positive and even useful aspects. Swallowers don't filter out their environment; instead, they tend to observe events receptively, absorb data, and record information. A swallower may serve well as the school's institutional memory. Swallowers often feel as though they observe life more than participate lending them well to recording the events in their environment.

In addition, people who fit this profile are receptive to mentoring and role modeling. As new teachers, they lap up the advice and support their mentors offer; as experienced teachers, they are good candidates to oversee a mentoring program, because they value its worth.

The Projector

Parker complains to Peg about a student in his seventh grade biology class. "We're studying the reproductive system and this one kid laughs every time I point to a diagram of the female anatomy. It's like dealing with a kindergarten student." He goes on to relate some of the bad jokes the student has launched, which somehow the other students find hilarious. "It's pointless to waste class time on this unit—his immaturity is spinning the class out of control."

When Peg tries to offer strategies that have worked for her in similar situations, he dismisses them: "That won't work," or "I've already tried it." Peg begins to get the feeling that his reluctance to help the kids work through their embarrassment stems in part from his own embarrassment—but he angrily rejects this suggestion as well. Frustrated, she finally gives up on her colleague.

Nobody likes to feel inadequate or incompetent—but what teacher will deny that teaching, more than other professions, highlights a person's shortcomings easily and often? Every classroom holds its challenges. It takes an open mind to identify the source of each challenge, and honesty to acknowledge that you yourself may be the source. Projectors prefer to place the blame elsewhere. If they can't connect with a student, they label the student as unreachable. If they can't solve a problem, they don't really want to hear how someone else has dealt with it better. If a situation threatens to reveal their inadequacies, they find a reason to bail out. They don't admit their own undesirable traits; instead, they project them onto others.

People like this often struggle to form meaningful and balanced relationships. They see others not as unique individuals with wants and needs of their own, but only as potential supporters or threats. They don't welcome feedback; instead, they seek out those who will tell them what they want to hear. At worst, they blame others for their own mistakes. They're not the most approachable or pleasant folks to work with, so they tend to be socially isolated—but they blame that on others too.

On the other hand, the fact that projectors often direct their attention and energy outward rather than inward can have its advantages. Their intuition of others can help provide stimulus for creative change. And if given the support they crave, they are independent enough to—on their own—meet the challenges they face.

The Reflector

Ruth, an elementary school special education teacher, was recently informed of a statewide curriculum change to standardize reading material. Ruth is concerned; her students already have difficulty keeping up, and this change may make it nearly impossible for them. She knows how easily her students lose confidence. How can she ask them to do work that is beyond their ability?

Even though she knows the decision is not likely to be modified, she hopes to be given some flexibility in order to meet the special needs of her students. She prepares a few specific examples to bring to her principal's attention: Some of her students do not know how to write a full sentence; how can they write a letter to their congressman about an issue they believe in? Some don't sit still for more than thirty seconds at a time without hitting or teasing their neighbors; how can they mentor each other without her input?

When she approaches her principal to discuss the issue, an argument ensues. The principal makes some hurtful comments—but she's the boss, so Ruth suppresses her angry retorts. Now the interpersonal conflict generates an intrapersonal conflict as well.

Ruth is caught between two strong emotions—anger at the principal's comments and fear of retaliation if she expresses the anger. Because she hasn't acted on either one, the standoff between these two competing energies causes turmoil. Such conflicts, if they occur on a regular basis, can create powerful disturbances within the body. Those who primarily employ the reflective style are prone to migraines and anxiety in the short term and more serious physiological problems in the long term.

Those who turn conflict inward, absorbing its effects, can benefit the organization. These people tend to control their impulses, helping to prevent hasty decisions that may be regretted later. Such people tend to be more diplomatic, acting as negotiators among their peers. At a time when schools are working hard to help children become more thoughtful and less impulsive in their behavior, reflectors may serve as good role models.

The Deflector

Everyone likes Debbie—sweet, cheerful, good-natured Debbie. Looking for someone to cover your class? Ask Debbie. Need a good lesson plan for your evaluation? Debbie will give you hers and write a new one for her own evaluation. Debbie even tended a student's pet lizard for three weeks because he thought his parents wouldn't let him keep it—and Debbie finds lizards repulsive. All her colleagues agree that Debbie is almost too good to be true. How does she do it?

Well, let's take a look. Debbie's principal has just put her on the hot seat—a regrettable tactic he uses to embarrass one teacher in order to "teach the faculty a lesson." Of course, Debbie rarely deserves such attention, but this year she has put off the classroom observation required for her annual evaluation. Time after time, she made excuses; in fact, she called in sick on both days when an observation loomed.

As the rest of the faculty looks on, the principal confronts Debbie. She replies politely, almost deferentially, avoiding eye contact. The principal presses harder. Though clearly uncomfortable, Debbie does not stiffen up; at most, she seems to be smirking, or even giggling. Like a martial artist evading her opponent's blows, Debbie artfully dodges each statement or question from her principal. None of his attacks get through her shield.

Deflectors, too, can make positive contributions to their school. When a conflict arises, a deflector can divert its negative energy. Deflectors provide a useful balance to the intensity of other faculty members who take everything very seriously.

The Merger

After years as principal of a small suburban middle school, Melanie is very interested in a promotion. Someday she wants to work for the board of education in an administrative capacity, perhaps as assistant superintendent. For now, her objectives include keeping on the superintendent's good side to ensure a positive recommendation. She works hard to cooperate with her boss; she knows that he values loyalty and cooperation even more than good job performance.

One might consider this strategy appropriate; in some school districts, disagreeing with the superintendent amounts to insubordination. But Melanie takes the same approach with most people, in most situations. She rarely turns down a request from her subordinates. She seldom challenges district policies and directives. Within her school, she doesn't clearly state what she wants teachers to do; instead, she drops hints or gives indirect messages. When she does implement changes, they originate from the faculty or support staff. Her primary goal is to be well thought of—that's what she believes makes a strong leader.

Melanie's husband, a successful attorney, works long hours. Their lack of intimacy concerns her, but she does nothing to rock the boat. She spends time with her two teenage daughters and their friends. She doesn't have any friends of her own; she blames that on her commitments to work and family.

In short, Melanie lacks self-definition. Outside her roles of principal, wife, and mother, she has no clear identity. In each relationship, she merges herself with the other. It's as if she takes up no space of her own. Eventually, she will feel lost—estranged from herself as well as from others.

And yet mergers exert creative forces too. They carry out directives reliably; they establish and maintain stability. Their gift for empathy makes them easy to get along with. They tend to do well in school systems because they tolerate change and uncertainty; where individuality is not encouraged, mergers make loyal followers.

The Desensitizer

Sally is having a hard year as principal. A raft of policy changes imposed by the district includes standardizing the curriculum—a project that her teachers find frustrating because they can't agree on how to implement the details. Faculty meetings have become increasingly tense and confrontational.

In a conversation with a close friend, Sally talks about her efforts to deal with the mounting tension. "I can't let it get to me—I have to find a way to lighten the mood," she says. "I'll bet you tell some great jokes," her friend responds. She's right; Sally relies on humor—along with a host of other creative responses—to relieve the pressure of a tense situation. Conflict causes anxiety; to minimize the anxiety in her life, Sally works hard to minimize conflict in her relationships.

Each of us can control the intensity of our interactions with others. It's as if we have a built-in dimmer switch that modulates the strength of the stimuli we take in and the vigor of our response. If the incoming signal seems too loud, we turn it down. If our own reaction feels too powerful we mute it.

Desensitizers like Sally continuously turn down their dimmer switch, even when they may not need to. In effect, they become masters at tuning out static, maintaining their balance. If external stimuli threaten to overload their system, they will take stronger measures, as if tripping an internal circuit breaker to cut off contact entirely.

In adopting this mode of interaction, desensitizers take charge of their relationships. Rather than expecting sensitivity or thoughtfulness from others, they alone decide what to let in. Instead of confronting others directly when they infringe on boundaries, desensitizers back away. In leadership positions, desensitizers set the parameters for how people relate; they control the amount and quality of contact between teachers and students, administrators and parents, teachers and administrators, and so on.

But contact—the connection between people when they experience each other as unique and separate individuals—brings depth to relationships. This real experience, whether it takes the form of agreement, understanding, recognition, or disgust, allows people to grow closer to one another. Contact creates the bonds of intimacy in a family, cohesion among a faculty. Even more than the shared experience of success, the resolution of conflict brings people together. When a desensitizer interrupts contact to minimize conflict, superficiality often takes its place.

What do desensitizers add to their environments? First, they have a definite calming effect, moderating the intensity of stressful situations or relieving pressure with a note of appropriate levity. Second, they keep their cool in emotionally charged moments. Not easily flustered, they bring a thoughtful and levelheaded approach to bear on issues that might otherwise escalate—an invaluable quality for the school setting.

Summary

+ Swallowers choke down feelings in order to prevent conflict—a response that may lead to physical problems over time. Swallowers retain information well and are receptive to mentoring and role modeling.

+ Projectors attribute their thoughts, feelings and beliefs to others rather than taking ownership of them. They tend to blame others for their own failings. Projectors may inspire creativity in others by focusing on them or intuiting about them in a way that draws out energy.

♦ Reflectors experience competing energies (forces for sameness and change) as turmoil. Those who rely on reflection can suffer migraines, anxiety, and eventually more serious physiological problems. However, their thoughtful self-control and diplomacy can yield advantages.

♦ Deflectors resist unpleasant feedback, dodge attacks, sidestep criticism, and generally avoid controversy and conflict.

♦ Mergers take on the attitudes of those around them rather than exerting a strong identity of their own. They empathize well with others and tolerate change and uncertainty.

♦ Desensitizers guard their own sensitivities. When others infringe on their boundaries, they react not by confrontation but by backing away or limiting contact.

Part III

Approaching Resistance

5

Typical Ways
of Dealing with
Resistance

I reserve the right to resist your attempts to influence me, and I reserve the right to try to overcome your resistance to my attempts to influence you.

a high school principal

The secretaries in the front office, the teachers and students in the classrooms, the principal who roams the halls—all are individuals with their own agendas, their own wants and needs. Inevitably, these come into conflict. The principal asks her secretary to finish the weekly newsletter—but the secretary had planned to leave early to watch her daughter's soccer game. A teacher wants to read his class a ballad—but the children have sat still all morning and need to wiggle. A principal schedules a staff development activity on the very day teachers must turn in their final grades. What happens next? Does it matter?

If the faculty members resentfully attend the in-service activity, how much will they gain from it? If the students don't listen to the ballad, has the teacher really met his objective? The secretary may finish the newsletter, but the principal has sacrificed the relationship for the outcome.

Some school leaders measure success in terms of attaining goals—checking off the objectives listed in performance improvement plans, reaching specified targets for student achievement, meeting the targets of individual education plans. People in the higher echelons of school systems reinforce this attitude by assessing performance in terms of measurable results. But if we focus on outcomes without noticing what happens along the way, we pay a price.

In particular, we need to notice what happens when we encounter resistance. In this chapter, we explore three common reactions to resistance:

◆ Overpowering

◆ Avoiding

◆ Circumventing

As you read these examples, consider how you tend to respond when resistance interferes with your agenda and blocks the path to your goal. Explore the price you pay.

Overpowering

Mrs. Overton ordinarily announced quizzes and tests ahead of time and held review sessions the day before. One April morning, she simply handed her seventh graders a multiple-choice chapter test. Their responses ranged from wide-eyed incredulity to stunned confusion, but as their agitation subsided, most of them turned their attention to the paper on their desk.

Only Jeff raised his hand to question this abrupt departure from the classroom routine.

Although he pleaded his case—their case—in a fairly appropriate manner, Mrs. Overton responded with stern severity, leaving no room for discussion or negotiation. "Just take the test," she ordered.

In the end, none of the students did very well on the test. Perhaps their grades reflected a lack of preparation, but other forces may have contributed as well. Surely other students shared Jeff's resistance to the situation; surely they shared his dismay when his protest went unheard. They may not have intentionally sabotaged the test results, but surely they approached the task with less concentration and less motivation to do well.

In this instance, Mrs. Overton made decisions based on her own agenda, tried to maintain control of the situation, and reacted instinctively when she encountered resistance. The schedule was tight; she needed to administer the chapter test that day, and she didn't 'have time' to discuss the matter or address her students' concerns.

Those initiating change often feel this sense of urgency. They have a goal in mind; they feel responsible for achieving it, the sooner the better. In an era of multitasking, teachers and school administrators find simple solutions very attractive. If every decision requires ongoing collaboration and consensus, exhaustion can set in.

It's tempting to charge ahead, quelling any opposition in our path. We may view resistance as a barrier or impediment; at a deeper level, resistance threatens our sense of power and control. But when we use force to thwart resistance, we invariably trigger unforeseen consequences—and these may even keep us from achieving our intended outcome.

If you find yourself routinely trying to overpower resistance, you may ask yourself why. What need does it satisfy? How does it work? How does this approach fit into your long-term goals, not merely your short-term objectives? What effect does it have on the climate of the school?

If you are ready to experiment with a new approach, consider allowing others to express their resistance and allowing yourself to explore its implications. How does the prospect make you feel? Do you fear losing control? Applaud yourself for recognizing this; you have begun important work in your role as a leader, facilitator, or organizer.

Avoiding

A well-heeled donor offered a Michigan middle school funding to support a web page to enhance communication between teachers and parents. Teachers could post lesson plans, homework assignments, calendar items, even models of student work that met standards. The principal, Mr. Caspar, initially welcomed the idea, but many faculty members had doubts. The technology coordinator knew this meant a lot of extra work for her; the sixth grade math teacher worried that the parents would find fault with the curriculum; the assistant principal hesitated to put the internal workings of the school under such a spotlight.

Rather than accepting the offer right away, Mr. Caspar formed a faculty committee to study the proposal. The committee met in June; the chairman presented its report to the principal within a week. The papers lay on his desk all summer. At the opening faculty meetings in September, one committee member inquired about the status of the proposal. Immediately, a heated debate erupted. Hemming and hawing, Mr. Caspar scheduled a meeting with the committee for the following week—but when the time came, a scheduling conflict arose and he missed the meeting.

To make a long story short, the principal put off any decision for a full year. By the time he finally consented to the proposal, the donor had withdrawn the offer.

Conflicts often promote discomfort; the need to negotiate or collaborate with people whose views differ from ours may trigger uncomfortable emotions, from irritation to frustration or even anger. We may deal with these emotions by not dealing with them. Rather than expressing our dissatisfaction or trying to work through the standoff, we simply transfer our energy and attention to other less contentious matters.

School leaders who routinely meet resistance with avoidance risk creating a climate where guardedness and self-protection prevail. Subordinates—teachers, support staff, students—come to feel that their concerns don't matter. At first, they find this frustrating; as the pattern of avoidance continues, their attitudes shift to resentment and finally to passive aggression and indifference. They invest less energy into their work; they detach themselves from issues that matter. The school just drifts along.

Circumventing

Mr. Hall complained to his principal, Mrs. Marks, that their high school was not doing enough to prevent fights from occurring outside the school. Mrs. Marks explained that because the fights took place after school hours and off school grounds, the school bore no responsibility. Dissatisfied with that response, Mr. Hall announced that he would send letters home to the parents of all his students to make them aware of the situation. In addition, he planned to call a friend at the local police department for help.

Without saying anything more to Mr. Hall, Mrs. Marks went to the superintendent and insisted that she stop him from taking any action. That week, the three parties met in the principal's office to review district policies and procedures.

In this instance, Mrs. Marks tolerated Mr. Hall's initial complaint but not his reaction to her response. He resisted the forces for sameness—her idea that the school should do nothing more to stop fights—by mobilizing and intensifying the forces for change. The principal chose to circumvent that resistance. As their disagreement escalated, she challenged Mr. Hall's plans indirectly. Whether she viewed the matter as irreconcilable, sought to avoid a power struggle, or simply did not know how to negotiate the issue, she turned to the superintendent to gain the outcome she wanted.

We may experience resistance as competition. We may hesitate to engage in a power struggle because we fear the other party will prevail. We may be unwilling to negotiate because we anticipate that we will give in. In that case, we may look for a way around the resistance. We may choose to make an end run around our opponents or otherwise sabotage their plans.

If school leaders habitually deal with resistance by circumventing it, they set the stage for a survival-of-the-fittest mentality. Members of the school community learn to resort to indirect measures to ensure that their needs are met. An atmosphere of suspicion and distrust prevails.

Summary

- Overpowering resistance often results in power struggles, stratification of faculty and students, and increased tension within a school system.

- People who dislike conflict typically meet resistance by avoiding it. When a leader chooses avoidance, subordinates feel that their concerns don't matter. As a result, they invest less energy into their own work.

- When people believe that a power struggle or even negotiation will lead to an undesirable outcome, they may circumvent resistance, taking an indirect route to achieve the outcome they want.

6
Working with Resistance

In the first four chapters, we explored the nature of resistance, outlining its origins and expression. In chapter five, we examined a few common reactions to resistance and noted the problems these can cause. In this chapter, we introduce novel ways of relating to and working with resistance.

The Paradoxical Theory of Change

As a first step to navigating this complex sea, let's take a look at an important concept about how people change. Paradoxically,

- People (or systems, or organizations) cannot move from one state of being to another until they have fully experienced or accepted their present state.

- People may need to examine the *objections to* doing something new before they can appreciate the *reasons for* doing it.

- Often, those who seek to initiate change must temporarily set aside their own investment in reaching the proposed outcome.

- Pressing for the outcome merely solidifies resistance to it, promoting opposition and preventing balance.

What does this theory of change look like in school situations? How does it play out in our relationships with colleagues, with subordinates, with parents, with students? Here are a few examples.

Experience the Present State

When a student complains of an upset stomach, the school nurse may call the parent and recommend over-the-counter remedies. These may bring temporary relief, but they do little to address possible underlying issues and tensions. With more insight, we might view such symptoms as messages from the body and take time to investigate the worries in the child's life as a possible cause. Ideally, we would pay attention not just to the surface, but to deeper levels of need as well.

Mrs. Roth believed that another member of the ninth grade team was undermining her relationship with their students. Angry letters of appeal to the principal brought no relief. Finally, Mrs. Roth sought coaching to help her let go of her anger and get on with her work. Under coaching, she found that she could not ignore her anger or sweep it aside. Before she could move forward, she had to fully examine her anger, experience it with curiosity instead of disdain or dread, and learn more about its origins. As she began to identify other feelings, such as loss and fear, her anger slowly dissipated and she could begin the hard work of acceptance.

Sam refused to do homework. All year, Mrs. Carey pushed, pulled, and even implored him to cooperate. Parent conferences, loss of privileges, and failing grades had no effect. At last, Mrs. Carey took Sam aside and said, "I give up. I only wish I understood why you won't do the work—not for me, but for yourself." Sam's response: "I don't want you to stop trying. It's the only time anybody pays attention to me."

Two things have happened here. First, Mrs. Carey abandoned the effort to make Sam meet her agenda. Schoolwork often represents the teacher's agenda, not the child's. Children, especially those with less hope of academic advancement, often care more about family problems, fitting in with friends, and other such issues than about the demands of academia.

Second, Mrs. Carey gained insight into Sam's deeper need. He craved attention—and his refusal to do homework drew attention from all sides. Armed with this understanding of his resistance, she could begin to draw him toward more adaptive behavior.

Principals and teachers who understand the importance of exploring the present can learn to view resistance as an opportunity for growth. When others don't behave as we expect, we can go beyond simply repeating our expectations, insisting on cooperation, and forging ahead toward our goals. If we explore resistance, we may reveal hidden assumptions and underlying implications. If we do this in company with others, walking alongside them rather than pushing or pulling, we may find that they view us as allies, not adversaries, on the road toward personal and professional growth.

Explore the Objections First

Mrs. Appleton informed her class they would begin staying after school three times a week for SAT prep. When they protested, she gave each student a chance to explain their objections. Some had sports practice; others listed family obligations, such as babysitting; still others wondered how they would find transportation home from school. Mrs. Appleton listened calmly, showing that she understood. Gradually, as the protests began to fade, one student commented that staying late for SAT prep might improve his prospects for college admission. One by one, other students began to recognize the importance of this extra time; one student even acknowledged that Mrs. Appleton would be staying late too! Eventually, most of the class could see how this temporary sacrifice would benefit them in the long run. Except for a few with unavoidable scheduling conflicts, most managed to attend the sessions.

By allowing her students to voice their objections, Mrs. Appleton let them work through their own resistance. Her calm neutrality helped them focus on the issue at hand rather than on a power struggle.

What makes it hard for leaders to allow the free expression of opposition? Perhaps we fear that one negative comment will trigger others; perhaps we fear opening the floodgates to a tide that will wash away our plans. Either outcome is less likely if a competent facilitator keeps the conversation flowing—helping people to hear themselves think, and leading them to consider in a new light the plan they oppose.

Often, we perceive objections to change as a decision not to cooperate, rather than as pragmatic or philosophical considerations in need of exploration. But the very act of examining objections can reduce their force. Conversely, our refusal to listen to others makes us the target of their resistance. Exploring the objections first can open the door to a very different result.

Set Aside Investment in the Outcome

Mrs. Carey very much wanted Sam to do his homework. Mrs. Appleton cared enough about improving her students' performance on the SAT to give up her own free time. But neither was able to reach her goal without setting aside—for a time—her own investment in the outcome.

The thought of holding our wants and needs in abeyance runs counter to our survival instincts. The idea of temporarily setting our objectives aside may not mesh with our drive for achievement, for success, for rewards—even for checking off tasks on our to-do list. It's easy to forget that achieving one objective may interfere with another outcome; eliminating one problem may give rise to three others.

Putting aside your investment in the outcome long enough to really hear and appreciate the objections of your subordinates can help them feel valued. If they feel valued they may become more receptive to what you have to say.

Don't Reinforce Opposition

Suppose that Mrs. Appleton had pushed her students to comply. Some might have simply skipped out; others might have brought their parents into the fray. The SAT prep sessions might have taken place in an atmosphere of stubborn resentment that interfered with learning and spilled over into the rest of the day.

Mrs. Appleton took a different tack. She viewed her students' resistance as a natural (but temporary) reaction to change. Rather than pushing back, thus establishing opposition as the normal state of tension, she waited and listened.

Rather than identifying her students as obstinate or diffi-cult—a label they would naturally reject—she respected their position and their needs. If she had forced them into a corner, they would have viewed her as an adversary and hardened their stance. Instead, she gave them room to explore the situa-tion and move to a new situation of balance.

Reframing Resistance

Some readers—especially those with years of experience in management—may still think of resistance as a force that blocks progress or slows down productivity. The word *resis-tance* still carries negative connotations, conjuring up vivid memories of questions, disagreements, conflicts, and foot-dragging. In this section, we'll attempt to replace those images with concrete *positive* impressions. As Watzlawick et al. (1974) wrote, "resistance can be turned into an important vehicle for change…by reframing the resistance as a precondi-tion for, or even an aspect of, change." We'll explore three ways to expand our appreciation for resistance and unlock its potential:

- ♦ Reframe resistance as *multidirectional energy*—forces or desires that pull in different directions, not all of which support each other.
- ♦ View this multidirectional energy as malleable and time-sensitive.
- ♦ Encourage the expression of feelings to identify the origin and direction of specific forces or desires.

With these ideas in mind, put yourself in the shoes of a high school principal in the following three scenarios.

Multidirectional Energy as Acceptable

You stop by the social studies department meeting to an-nounce a plan to purchase new books. As you ask the teachers to submit their choices by Thursday, one shakes her head in disapproval. With twelve other appointments on your schedule, you're tempted to ignore her signal, but you recognize the importance of process over content.

Principal: I can see that you have some concerns about what I just said.

Teacher: I'm just not sure we'll have time to meet your deadline.

Principal: Actually, it's not my deadline; it's the district deadline. They plan to pool the orders to get a discount.

Teacher: Why didn't anybody tell us about this sooner?

At this point, you may feel like hurling an eraser at the teacher. After all, you're not trying to make her job more difficult—in fact, you're giving her department complete control over a decision that directly affects her. Why doesn't she appreciate that?

Instead, you pause to consider the nature of the teacher's resistance. You recognize her resentment; you only received this request today, and the short notice irritated you as well. You visualize the teacher's dismay not as opposition, but as a force pulling in a direction away from your objective—like the vectors you studied in a long-ago math class. You recognize its energy and respond appropriately.

Principal: I know this deadline is tight, especially with everything else you have going on. This will probably end up as another task you take home to do on your own time—and believe me, I appreciate that. Let me know if I can help in any way.

Give yourself a pat on the back. You managed to reframe resistance as multidirectional energy. Instead of fighting it, you respected its force and accepted it gracefully.

Multidirectional Energy as Malleable and Time-Sensitive

You send the faculty a memo announcing that this year's schedule for parent-teacher conferences will allow only five minutes with each parent. One teacher stops you in the hall to discuss the new policy.

> Teacher: You know what's going to happen, don't you? Some parents are going to be very upset when we cut them off. I can see that the new schedule gives us a chance to talk with every parent, but it's going to cause quite a stir.

You recognize that this teacher has mixed feelings about the anticipated change. She hasn't challenged the decision or refused to cooperate, but you detect a certain level of tension. Now, you could minimize her concerns, engage in a dispute, or dismiss her comments entirely. Instead, you visualize her ambivalence as two forces pulling her in different directions. Furthermore, you know that such forces can coexist—but only for a period of time. One or another will eventually prevail. You take advantage of this window of opportunity to influence the outcome.

> Principal: This change brings benefits we haven't talked about, but I certainly see the added problems you mention. We don't want to upset the parents, especially the ones we need the most time with, but I also don't want you teachers here until midnight. Would it help if I notified the parents of this change in advance? Or perhaps you have another suggestion.

> Teacher: No, that's okay. I think the parents of my students will understand if I explain that they can contact me any time during the semester to schedule a longer meeting.

Once again, give yourself credit. By recognizing the teacher's point, remembering that initial resistance may change over time, and by stepping in to shape that resistance, you have just avoided an unnecessary power struggle and continued toward your goal.

Multidirectional Energy as Informative

A new district policy requires you to observe each teacher in the classroom setting at least once each quarter. When you announce the change, the faculty meeting simmers with signs of displeasure—from sighs and raised eyebrows to a ripple of grumbles. Nobody voices their feelings directly, and you're tempted to just move on. But you value open communication, so you initiate a dialogue.

Principal: I get the impression that many of you have strong feelings about this, and I'm interested in hearing them.

Teacher 1: It's just one thing after another! We've already lost too much class time for standardized tests and test prep.

Principal: I know it feels like one more added pressure. You must be worried about how to fit it all in.

Teacher 2: Will we get any notice for these observations, or will you just spring them on us?

Principal: We'll work together to schedule them. Believe me, I understand how it feels to have someone drop in for an unexpected classroom observation!

Teacher 3: I don't know why we have observations anyway—they don't serve any purpose but to give us heart palpitations.

By encouraging these teachers to express their feelings directly, you have zeroed in on the source of their resistance. It probably wouldn't matter how many observations you scheduled or how much advance notice they had—it's the observation itself that creates anxiety and trepidation. Now you can work with the teachers to make these sessions less traumatic and more helpful.

Polarities

♦ A principal decides to give the faculty greater autonomy in choosing their curriculum. Some teachers favor this increased freedom; others worry about the lack of support or guidance.

♦ An assistant principal changes the bus schedule. Some parents can let their children sleep fifteen minutes later; others must set their alarms half an hour earlier.

♦ The fifth grade team leader switches a student from one reading group to another. One teacher feels relief; another faces a new challenge.

Principals and other school leaders often feel that they can't win: No matter what they do, they will upset somebody. As middle managers, they make decisions that disturb the equilibrium of the system. A change in one area affects the situation elsewhere. A plan that pleases some people leaves others dissatisfied—and distresses still others. No doubt you can think of any number of vivid examples.

What does it mean when people within a group—a family, an organization, a school— disagree? We can look at this common occurrence in two ways. We could view one position as right and the other as wrong. The plan makes sense, or it doesn't; the proposal will work, or it won't; the decision has merit, or it doesn't. This either/or approach considers the forces at work as separate and unrelated. Opposites compete. Diversity leads to fragmentation. Resistance poses a threat.

Or we could choose a different perspective. We could view opposites as polarities—the two extremes of a continuum, like the positive and negative poles of an electrical field. In this view, opposing forces don't compete; rather, they form complementary parts of one integral whole. They shed light on each other; they work together. This approach welcomes diversity and regards resistance as a creative force that helps maintain equilibrium.

Think of an organization as an oceangoing vessel—never perfectly balanced, but constantly righting itself to one side or the other as the wind and waves exert their forces. As the captain of the ship, your job is to assess those forces and keep the ship steady as you steer your course.

The decisions you make also alter the ship's balance—in both intended and unintended ways. Resistance can alert you to the unintended consequences of change. The prudent leader respects the force of resistance and explores it with curiosity.

No change meets with total support on all sides—but leaders who identify the forces for and against change as parts of a continuum can steer a course toward coherence rather than fragmentation. When you feel as though you can't win, stop and think not of winning and losing, but of maintaining balance—and welcome resistance as a valuable force.

The Value of Resistance

What might we value about the resisters in our midst?

Resisters Seek to Protect the System's Integrity and Core Values

Every established organization has its "old guard"—the individuals who take it upon themselves to preserve the integrity of its culture. Countering risk-taking, spontaneity, and chaos with conservation, thoughtfulness, and order, this loyal element moderates the pace and intensity of change.

Consider a school that repeatedly tinkers with the class schedule. A traditional seven-period day gives way to a block schedule, then a modified block plan. Semester courses replace yearlong courses, then yield to trimesters. Would it surprise you to hear that yet another revamping of the schedule would encounter resistance?

Change doesn't necessarily bring improvement. Why didn't the old ways work? Did they fall victim to faulty planning? Lack of effort or motivation? Poor communication? Organizational lapses? Unanticipated roadblocks? Unless these problems are addressed, a new approach will probably lead to the same results. Doing things differently is no guarantee of doing things well.

Those who resist change often value what has worked well in the past (though they look with disfavor on the recycling of what has not). Occasionally, a resister serves as the lone watchdog for a particular program or tradition, jealously guarding it against gradual decline or sudden dismantling. Such resisters likewise seek to maintain the integrity of the school as they came to appreciate it.

Resisters help keep a school on track. For instance, a school that values sensitivity to diversity will want its leaders to evaluate any proposed organizational change with that in mind. The more closely a school abides by its espoused values, the greater its integrity—and the less the likelihood of resistance to change within that framework. Schools that stray from their purported values may encounter a higher level of mistrust, suspicion, and resistance to change. Resisters often have sensitive antennae for changes that lack what Jane Bluestein (2001) calls congruence—the matching of practices to goals.

Resisters See Consequences That the Initiators of Change Have Not Anticipated and That May Threaten the System's Well Being

Twenty years ago, to ease the overcrowding of schools across the borough, Staten Island built a large high school complete with spacious grounds, modern sports facilities, even artistic sculptures. Fifteen years later, the school population was down by half, athletic teams had dwindled, graffiti covered the walls, and cigarette butts littered the grounds. Nobody could have predicted the demographic changes in the school community that led to this transformation— but many along the way had voiced concerns about misguided objectives, failed experiments, and other decisions that whittled away at the school's core. Veteran teachers, looking back, expressed frustration and regret that their resistance went unheeded.

A rock tossed into still water sends out ripples in a smooth circular pattern. In schools, every change disturbs the calm differently, depending upon the resistance encountered and the response to that resistance. Those who seek to initiate change would do well to heed the ripples on the water.

Resisters React Particularly to Changes They View as Reducing the Self-esteem, Competence, or Autonomy of Individuals Within the System

As a cost-cutting measure to relieve local and state budgets, the New Jersey state assembly proposed legislation to promote early retirement of teachers. The state board of education vigorously resisted the move, arguing that the loss of experienced teachers would diminish the quality of schools as learning environments.

Fiscal responsibility is an important consideration—but not the only important consideration. Furthermore, those who question a proposed change are not always mavericks or nay sayers; often, they include people with the power to make (or at least influence) decisions. Resisters help to balance the needs of the system against the needs of individuals.

Summary

♦ The paradoxical theory of change describes a dynamic process that depends on an understanding of *what is* and emphasizes balance over opposition or outcomes.

♦ Reframing resistance as multidirectional energy opens the door to exploration and shaping of the forces for and against change.

♦ Polarities represent the two extremes of a continuum within which different forces complement and balance each other.

♦ Resistance as a creative force moderates change, protects established values, and helps balance the needs of the individual against those of the organization.

Suggested Reading

Bluestein, J. (2001). *Creating emotionally safe schools*. Deerfield Beach, FL: Health Communications.

Nevis, Edwin D. (2001). Organizational consulting: A Gestalt perspective. Cambridge, MA: Gestalt Press.

Watzlawick, P., Weakland, J., & Fisch, R. (1974). *Change: Principles of problem formation and problem resolution*. New York: W. W. Norton and Company.

7

Strategies for Success

Effective school reform cannot happen until people move be-
yond superficial conceptions of educational systems and rec-
ognize the unseen values and attitudes about power, privi-
lege, and knowledge that keep existing structures, regula-
tions, and authority relationships in place. If there aren't
fundamental shifts in how people think and interact, as well
as in how they explore new ideas, then all of the reorganizing,
fads, and strategies in the world won't add up to much.

Peter Senge

We've all read about a host of techniques and strategies for
dealing with colleagues, subordinates, and students. Perhaps
we've tried one or another, with limited success. Often, our attempts have faltered because we didn't really understand the
behaviors we tried to address, or appreciate the systemic influences that made intervention necessary.

In these pages, you have read about the theoretical under-
pinnings of a different approach to resistance. Now it's time to
focus on the practical applications of this theory.

In this chapter, we'll set forth examples of just a few essential tools. You may recognize some of these from other settings;
after all, they represent good "people skills." But perhaps you'll
see them in a different light as a natural outcropping of the
philosophical beliefs outlined in earlier chapters.

Primary Tools

When you encounter resistance, your response matters. The
way you treat others at this important moment will do much to
determine the course of events. Here, we describe three key behaviors that promote healthy adaptation to change.

Empathize with the Individual or Group

Teacher: If this child isn't removed from my class immediately, I'll complain to the school board. He's disrupting the whole classroom.

Principal: I've never seen you this upset before. Please tell me what's going on.

Teacher: Today's incident was the last straw. This child has no limits. He thinks he can do whatever he wants and nobody will do anything about it.

Principal: Have we sent him a message that he can get away with unruly behavior?

Teacher: Well, the last time he broke the rules we suspended him, and now, two weeks later, he's back to his old nonsense.

Principal: Okay, I hear you. Having this student in your class makes it very difficult to work with the rest of your students. If we discipline him and it doesn't have any effect, then you're worried about what message that will send to others.

Teacher: You're right about that—I'm at my wits' end. We've got to find a way to deal with this.

The principal's empathy tempered the intensity of the teacher's reaction. Instead of getting into a debate about transferring the student, he began with an appreciation of her experience. This allowed her to move to a more thoughtful place where reasoning could take over.

Often, we hesitate to empathize because we don't want to give the impression that we agree with others or approve of their actions or beliefs. Some find it difficult to empathize because they truly cannot see beyond their own perspective; they believe that the only way to resolve a problem lies in getting the other person to acknowledge the "rightness" of their own view. Let's look at a scenario that illustrates this phenomenon.

Perspective 1

Anne is a fourth grade teacher, one of two in her school. Anne is very upset with her counterpart teacher, Grace, with whom she has collaborated for several years. The two have shared lesson plans, arranged to switch difficult students between classes, and even socialized outside of school. Now Anne feels that Grace has let her down. She had asked Grace to watch Timmy, a student who needed a "time out." After working with Timmy for several months regarding his impulse control, she was actually making headway, because she had earned his trust. The deal was that if he could follow through on certain tasks, she would give a positive report to his parents. Anne knew that Timmy was treated very harshly at home; she even suspected some mistreatment. When she learned that Grace had called Timmy's parents, she was furious. How could she not have checked in with her first? What right did Grace have to act so independently with one of her students? Anne feared that all her hard work with Timmy was out the window; furthermore, she worried about the child's safety.

Perspective 2

Grace had disciplined Timmy, a student she had been minding on "time out" at Anne's request. Grace was reluctant to take Timmy in to begin with, because she knew he was difficult to manage. She hadn't received any special instructions; Anne had merely asked her to keep him for the remainder of the day. When Timmy disrupted Grace's class, she reminded him several times that he needed to cooperate. When he became disrespectful, she sent him to the dean, who called his parents. Grace had tried to get in touch with Anne before sending him to the dean, but she was unavailable. She thought she would be doing Anne a favor by handling the incident herself, since she had agreed to give Anne a rest.

Either perspective has its merits. If you relate to one more than the other, ask yourself why; for example, perhaps you have had a similar experience. If you could see both perspectives equally, then you have taken something valuable from the exercise—the recognition that personal interactions rarely have clear rights and wrongs. Each perspective has its own important meaning. By empathizing, we can begin to investigate that meaning.

Empathizing helps us understand another person's experience or perspective, especially when it differs from our own. It doesn't imply that we agree; it simply shows that we care. We communicate this understanding through reflective listening—mirroring the other person's perspective. Without evaluating, agreeing, or disagreeing, we demonstrate that we have heard and understood what the other person is trying to say.

The skill of reflective listening is the single most useful item in a leader's toolbox. By using this tool appropriately, you can improve your relationships with colleagues, subordinates, and supervisors. Reflective listening can also make a difference in your personal relationships; how often have you heard your spouse, partner, or teenage daughter say, "You don't understand"? People who feel understood are less likely to maximize (exaggerate, intensify, magnify) their message and more likely to listen to another perspective.

Furthermore, reflective listening can help the person who sends a message to clarify its intended meaning:

Teacher: "I am really angry with you for the way you spoke with me yesterday."

Coworker: "Hmm…. You're angry with me."

Teacher: "Well, not so much angry as hurt."

In particular, our reflective listening can help students—young people who are still learning to express themselves—to practice and refine their articulation of thoughts and feelings.

Reflective listening demonstrates respect and helps build trust. When we take the time to listen, we help the other person feel valued. When we expend the energy to show our understanding, we establish a bond. Our dialogue deepens. Here is an example of that dynamic at work:

Teacher: You're saying you didn't turn in your homework because you didn't write down the assignment before you left for the day.

Student: I really meant to, but...I don't know, I guess I wasn't paying attention.

Teacher: You didn't forget on purpose; it sounds like you had a lot on your mind.

Student: I was thinking about a lot.

Teacher: You had a lot going on in your head.

Student: Well...between everything going on at home and then what happened at recess with the other kids...

In the previous chapter, we explored the benefits of reframing resistance as multidirectional energy. Reflective listening enables us to understand another person's perspective as a complementary position along a continuum between polarities, rather than as an opposing force. As we demonstrate that understanding and convey our sincere appreciation for the other person's experience, thoughts, and feelings, we open the door to dealing with resistance in a healthy way.

Teacher: It was a terrible idea to make this training mandatory. Not only does it interfere with a prep period that many of us were counting on, but also the topic of the workshop has nothing to do with our curriculum.

Principal: So, the timing is bad and the subject isn't relevant?

Teacher: It's not relevant at all. I don't understand why somebody doesn't ask us what would be useful. That would make a lot more sense.

Principal: I hear you—you would like more input into the decision-making process. Then at least

you could select topics that fit with what you are
doing.

Teacher: I know there are a lot of us, so it's not easy
to select a topic that fits for everyone. Sometimes
we will just have to grin and bear it.

Principal: Thank you for understanding how difficult it is to please everybody.

A word of caution: Reflective listening means more than
just parroting back what the other person says—a tactic that
comes across as pacifying or even patronizing. Reflective listening must be part of an authentic attempt to understand the
other person's perspective.

Empathy, gained through reflective listening, can help
transform a school from a "learning factory" where people
feel alone, alienated, and overburdened to a caring environment where each person feels listened to, appreciated, and
motivated. As school leaders, we can offer this gift to our
schools.

Describe Your Own Experience
When Appropriate

Teacher: Thanks for letting me vent about
Jimmy—but I'm still not convinced that having
him in my class is the best solution.

Principal: I know you're not thrilled about the idea,
but at the moment I'm not sure where else to put
him. Besides, I really think this challenge will be
good for you.

Teacher (laughs):   I'm not sure how you see me losing
my hair as a challenge.

Principal: When I was a teacher I had a similar situation with a student and I begged my principal to
get him out of my class.

Teacher: And I suppose you're going to tell me that
you were forced to keep the student and it turned
out for the best.

Principal: Well, yes—I was forced to keep the student, and I was miserable—but it didn't turn out well at all.

Teacher: I don't understand—then why do I have to keep Jimmy with me?

Principal (smiling): Well, if I had to suffer, then so do you. (Both laugh.)

While in this example self-disclosure was mixed with humor, it served the purpose of softening the teacher's resistance. The two might have continued the dialogue, discussing the teacher's experience in greater depth or exploring ways to work with young Jimmy. Like reflective listening, sharing a relevant personal experience demonstrates empathy and opens the door to problem solving. At the same time, a leader's self-disclosure to a subordinate helps to balance the power differential between the two, minimizing unnecessary resistance.

When we relate an experience that links us to others, we reframe resistance. Rather than isolating resisters, inducing them to protect their turf or gird themselves for conflict, we send the message that they don't need to be alone if they choose not to be.

However, sharing your own thoughts and feelings is not a desirable strategy for the early stages of conflict resolution. Before we ask others to take on our perspective, we must let them know that we understand theirs. This applies especially if they perceive us as responsible for the change they resist. We must also take care not to use self-disclosure as a means of manipulating others to gain their consent.

Model Healthy Adaptation

Many teachers know that principals, like most middle managers, receive directives and pressure from above. Often, principals must implement changes that are not of their own choosing. The way a principal responds to these imposed changes sets a model for others to follow. Some principals apparently believe that complaining about district mandates brings them closer to their faculty:

Principal: Well, they did it to us again. Prepare your-
  selves for the latest bright idea from our district.

Teacher: Now what?

Principal: It seems that in their infinite wisdom they
  have decided to ban bag lunches because they're a
  risk to public safety.

Teacher: I have to hear this one. How are bag
  lunches supposed to be a danger?

Principal: Did you read about the student in Califor-
  nia who brought a handgun to school in a brown
  paper bag? Well...

Teacher (in disbelief): So what are the parents supposed to do, give these kids money to buy lunch
  every day? What about the ones who can't afford
  that?

The way this principal presented the new policy did much
to determine the teacher's reaction. Presenting the district as
an antagonist may make the principal feel aligned with the
faculty, but in fact it sets a precedent for a pattern of opposition and resistance. In the long run, this approach may open
the door for others to view complaining or protesting as not
only proper but also necessary.

Principals and other leaders who can express their disagreement without deriding their superiors will earn the respect of their faculty and others in the school community.
Leaders who model an attempt to understand different perspectives set the stage for a healthier form of resistance and
enhance the school's ability to adapt to change.

Let's look at an alternative approach to the same situation:

Principal: The district has announced a change in
  policy, effective immediately. It may seem like an
  unusual request, but nonetheless it has to be done.

Teacher: What is it this time?

Principal: It seems that after recent events at another
  school involving gun possession, we are being
  asked to restrict lunches to cafeteria meals—no
  more bag lunches.

Teacher: What about those families that can't afford it? Are you saying they will have to buy lunch or not have any?

Principal: I know it may seem unfair to a good number of families, and perhaps like an overreaction to a random act not even close to here, but safety has got to be our highest priority. Maybe we can put our heads together and come up with some alternative ideas to present to the district.

Here, the principal doesn't indicate any agreement or disagreement with the directive. Withholding judgment, he expresses his understanding of the thinking behind the change as well as his willingness to address the problems it will create. He has modeled a healthy adaptation to change.

Secondary Tools

Empathy, self-disclosure, and modeling healthy adaptation set the stage for dealing with resistance to change. Now let's look at several more specific tactics for working through this process.

Draw out Resistance into the Open Where You Can Address it

By now, readers of this book surely recognize schools as potential hotbeds of resistance. In particular, experienced school leaders know how faculty members tend to respond to the prospect of change. Defenses go up; apprehension sets in. Like turtles drawing into their shells, people become closed in posture and in attitude. They may not hear all that we say; nuances may be lost or screened out.

Not everyone reacts this way, of course. Some people move easily with the flow of change, presenting little outward resistance. But even when resistance is not apparent, those who initiate change would do well to investigate the forces at work under the surface. "I appreciate your receptiveness to this change—but I would be very interested in hearing your concerns as well."

Some readers may resist this idea. Why open a can of worms? The answer is simple: Resistance is better dealt with in the open. We have seen that any proposed change triggers a range of responses along a continuum between extremes. Forces for sameness tug in one direction; forces for change pull in another direction. The captain of a ship wants to know where the underwater reefs lie, where the hidden currents run. Likewise, the prudent school leader wants to explore how others react to the prospect of change. A principal who demonstrates sensitivity to faculty concerns is more likely to win—and maintain—support than one who attends only to the forces flowing her way. A teacher who overlooks or dismisses the thoughts and feelings of his students is more likely to find them joining ranks in opposition to his or her power.

Identify the Source and Nature of Resistance

As we saw in chapter four, resistance takes various forms; people express their resistance differently depending on their individual personalities and particular situations. In Chapter five, we looked at typical ways of responding to resistance. In the following dialogue, a teacher expresses resistance and a principal responds. Read the dialogue first; consider your own reactions and jot down your thoughts about how resistance is expressed and managed. Then read the narrative on the right side, which links the described behavior to the styles described in chapter four and five.

Figure 7.1. Resistance Management

Dialogue	Interpretation
Principal: I'm glad you're here. I'd like to go over your annual evaluation, as we discussed. Teacher: I'm not sure we're going to have enough time—my students are due back from gym early. Principal: Well, let's see how much we can do in the time that we have. You have already seen your observation results, so this is not going to be very new to you.	The teacher begins to project her dismay onto the students, accusing them of sabotaging her evaluation.
Teacher: That was the worst possible day for an observation—it's as if the kids knew I was being evaluated and purposely decided to be at their worst.	The teacher begins to project her sense of frustration onto the students who "purposely" tried to sabotage her.
Principal: Well, as I told you that day, I thought you handled the children well. If you use reinforcement in addition to consequences, you may get better cooperation.	The principal begins by supporting the teacher, offering her praise. He immediately moves on to a suggestion that he made earlier, negating the positive affirmation that came before it. In essence, he is circumventing the resistance by making a suggestion.

Dialogue	*Interpretation*
Teacher: I started doing that the next day and it went much better. Your idea was more helpful than the others.	The teacher may be experiencing some discomfort at this point but elects to merge with her principal by taking on the advice, aligning herself with him.
Principal: And I told you how I feel about using students to grade each other's papers. I think it sends a message of laziness to the children. Teacher (looking at the floor): Uh-huh.	At this point, the teacher is likely feeling angry at the admonishment but also fearful of expressing herself. A reflector will generally demonstrate uneasiness physically rather than verbally, because of the conflict between emotions.
Principal: How are you doing with your mentor? Are you meeting with her regularly? Teacher: Yes—when time permits, we try to meet at least once a month.	The teacher then swallows her anger, telling the principal that she is attempting to follow procedures, even though she may be having a hard time with it.
Principal: I think it's important that you make it a priority. I matched you up with a very solid mentor who has very good control of her class. Teacher: Okay, I'll add it to the list of other priorities.	Through her use of sarcasm, the teacher is demonstrating the style of a desensitizer. She feels demeaned by the principal, so she takes the focus off herself by joking about being overwhelmed.
Principal: We need to go over a few other things, but they can wait until you have more time.	The principal avoids this resistance.

Match the Level of Intensity

Picture a novice sailor and an expert steering their respective crafts across the water. They encounter the same wind and waves, but only the expert leaves a straight and steady wake. The novice hasn't mastered the art of turning the tiller or adjusting the sails with just the right amount of force to match a sudden swell or a gust of wind.

School leaders who seek to steer a steady course must likewise learn to adjust their reactions to the forces they encounter. If a staff member expresses resistance with a sigh and a smile, a strong reaction might make the situation worse. A calm demeanor might soothe an irate teacher, but not if it suggests a total lack of interest.

Leaders have personalities too, of course, and the intensity of their reactions will reflect this. A mild-mannered principal will generally respond to resistance differently than one who is more high-strung. We've all seen how students learn to anticipate the way a particular teacher gives directives, establishes limits, or sets consequences. They take the intensity of our temperaments in stride.

However, we must recognize that those who work for us (or learn from us) tolerate differences in intensity less readily when resistance is an issue. Resistance arises when the prospect of change, or change itself, creates uncertainty and ambivalence. Under such circumstances, people feel vulnerable; this makes them more sensitive to the intensity of our reactions. With their protective mechanisms on high alert, they notice the tone, volume, and pitch of our message even more than its content.

With practice, we can learn to adjust the intensity of our response so that it reaches—but does not overwhelm—the resister. Like the expert sailor, we can respond to the forces of resistance with just enough intensity to maintain a steady forward course.

State Your Appreciation for the Way Others Experience Change

The prospect of change often triggers both anxiety and excitement. Questions arise about its impact as well as the process itself. How will the new policy affect my work? How will I be evaluated under the new system? What if I don't understand my role in the transition? What happens if I can't alter my procedures in the time required?

People experience these questions, this excitement and anxiety, as conscious and subconscious tension. As the person responsible for initiating or implementing change, you can alleviate much of this tension by developing a healthy dialogue that is open and honest—even if the answers to many of the questions are "I don't know."

Earlier in this chapter, we noted that disclosing your own feelings might also help—after you have listened to and acknowledged the concerns of others. Effective leaders strike a balance between inspiring confidence that they will guide the process with a strong hand and letting others know that their human reactions are shared.

The first step to appreciating the way others experience change is to understand their experience. As we have seen throughout this book, the work begins with curiosity: asking questions, encouraging honest disclosure, empathizing, and exploring the polarities of change. Along the way, you may genuinely acknowledge the impact that the intended change will have on the individual and the system. Remember that people will react to both the anticipated consequences of the change and the way change takes place.

Teacher: So, how is this going to affect our prep periods? I don't have enough time to get my work done as it is.

Principal: It must seem as if every change adds more work and nothing gets taken away.

Teacher: Exactly—you got that right.

Adjust Your Approach Depending upon Whether You Initiate the Change or it Comes from an Outside Source

When a change originates within your sphere of influence, you have the opportunity to involve the constituents of that change—the people responsible for implementing and sustaining it—in a significant way. The more involved the constituents, the greater their investment in the outcome; the more excluded, the greater their resistance.

If the change originates outside your sphere of influence (for example, from higher echelons), you won't have this option. In that case, your task is to help the people in your charge to adapt. This may involve allowing them to express anger, powerlessness, or the sense that they are not appreciated or respected. Give permission to share openly while recognizing your own feeling of being caught in the middle. Especially if you have no control over the imposed change, it would be unhealthy to expect yourself or others to go along with it silently. Keep in mind there is a difference between complaining and venting. Venting (when done directly and respectfully) is a more open expression of feeling that may lead to problem solving.

When you can influence the course of change, the process becomes more complex—but it also offers greater opportunities to manage resistance. Whenever possible, bring your constituents in at the earliest opportunity to maximize their investment. Of course, this means you will have more opinions and perspectives to consider; however, a solid understanding of group process and team building can help generate creativity out of the inevitable conflicts.

Once you have enlisted your constituents, continue to evaluate along the way. If there's no wiggle room about the outcome itself, try to be flexible about the way it's implemented. Recognize that other people will adapt your idea into something that reflects their own vision. Creating a shared picture is a wonderful way to unite and build your team.

As the person responsible for change, you will encounter more fervent resistance; people expect you to exercise greater sensitivity to their needs—and to give them more control over the circumstances of change—than they might demand from a remote and impersonal higher-up. It's best to acknowledge this desire for greater control, even if you don't intend to offer it. Be honest with yourself about why you don't want to involve others; as far as you are willing, let others know why too. The statement "I just don't have time or energy right now to make this a team project" may sound awkward, but honesty invites respect.

Pay Attention to Your Own Needs and Choices

Don't neglect this essential task. The captain of a sailing vessel must assess the forces of wind and waves, tend to the rudder and sails, and keep up the crew's morale—but over a long voyage, the captain must also eat and sleep and exercise. As a principal, a classroom teacher, or the leader of any other group, you must constantly react to the needs of other individuals and meet the needs of the organization—but you must consider your own needs as well.

Balancing these three forces demands strenuous effort; setting priorities becomes a confusing challenge. Many school leaders believe their primary responsibility is to the faculty and staff, or perhaps to the students, but your own needs are equally powerful and important. Unless your needs are met, you will not be able to satisfy those who rely on you.

This does not mean that your needs must be met immediately. Once you have clearly identified them, you define your own work and set your own schedule for meeting them. We have spoken of responding to resistance with empathy, but this does not mean closing off awareness of your own feelings, thoughts, perceptions, and reactions. Indeed, the more you acknowledge your own human needs, the more you are able to accept those of others.

Some of the choices you might make as a leader are not healthy either for you or for the system. If your inclination is to maintain a veneer of calm, you may decide not to explore resistance. If your tendency is to forge ahead toward your chosen outcome, you may impose your authority with fear as a motivator. Neither decision will eliminate dissent. Whether by sabotage, by gradual neglect, or by outright defiance, people will find a way to thwart your plans—and the organizational culture will suffer.

Like the captain of a ship at sea, you must maintain a vigilant self-awareness. Explore your responses to change in your own life. Pay attention to your tolerance for resistance and the ways you choose to manage it. Learn from your mistakes and applaud your successes. Most of all, find satisfaction in the voyage.

Summary

♦ Empathy is the single most important skill for leaders who seek respect and cooperation. By expressing understanding of another person's feelings, wishes, and beliefs, we build trust and improve relationships.

♦ Self-disclosure lets others know our own feelings and thoughts; this may help to reduce resistance.

♦ How we respond to resistance sets the tone for those who look up to us.

♦ Effective tactics for managing resistance include drawing it into the open, identifying its source and nature, matching its intensity, letting others know we value their experience, adjusting our approach, and practicing self-awareness.

Suggested Reading

Senge, P. (2000). *Schools that learn.* New York: Doubleday.

8

Effects of Working with Resistance

Throughout this book, you have been encouraged to explore alternative perspectives and experiment with new ways of managing resistance. You may not change your leadership style entirely, but as you reflect on its strengths and limitations, you may decide to incorporate new approaches that yield a better balance. This involves risk, of course—but transformation and growth require a certain amount of risk-taking. "If you continue to do what you have always done, you will get what you have always gotten" (Bates, 2001). I'd like to share with you an example from my own experience with risk-taking as an organizational leader.

Many years ago, as a consultant to a school in Canada, I met with the school principal (Lynda), the assistant principal (Jason), and several other key faculty members. Lynda had served as a school principal in the same district for thirteen years, and she had often skirmished with the faculty, but this year the battles seemed to rage nonstop. Jason worked very hard to remain neutral. At times he tried to act as a buffer between Lynda and the faculty, but that only brought complaints raining down on him from both sides. My efforts focused on getting each side to listen to the other's concerns, to see things from the other's perspective.

After about ten months, we agreed on only one thing: We all felt stuck. Neither the faculty nor the administration would agree to come together to address the issues; each insisted that it worked better for them to meet with me separately. The teachers particularly resisted a joint meeting; in my opinion, they feared that if they voiced their views openly, they would lose whatever support they had from Jason. Lynda continued to blame the teachers for the tension in the school; Jason felt caught in the middle.

I began to press Lynda to ease up on the teachers. I'd say, "If you want to drive a deeper wedge you can keep blaming—but if you want to improve relations, you had better start listening to their concerns." I could tell that she felt hurt by the way her teachers treated her; I also sensed that she felt some responsibility for the situation but resisted acknowledging this because of her hurt feelings. Though aware of this resistance, I pushed her to take my advice.

One day, I met with Lynda alone. Outraged, she told me that a teacher had defied her yet again. A student had misbehaved in class; in response, the teacher told his parents he couldn't go on the next class trip. This was against school policy, and the teacher knew it; she had argued with the principal about it just the week before. Lynda was at her wits' end—so desperate that she was ready to listen to any suggestions I had for her.

I seized the opportunity—but this time, I didn't try to tell her what to do. Instead, I encouraged her to explore her choices and her resistance to each option. "I know the whole situation seems hopeless; sometimes I get the sense you even blame yourself. I wonder what would happen if you reprimanded the teacher? What if you met with her to find out more about why she made this decision?"

From that point forward, Lynda began to let down her guard. Once she felt understood, she opened her mind to the possibility of understanding the teachers and their frustrations. We talked about her fear that the school district would blame her for failing to implement the very policies her teachers resisted. She wasn't eager to meet with the faculty, but she agreed to try it—and the faculty agreed as well.

The entire faculty met for the first time in several months, talking through their conflicts in a very professional manner. As consultant, I facilitated the meeting, encouraging each participant to take ownership of the issues and to demonstrate empathy. Teachers and administrators examined their roles in perpetuating the tension without either side feeling blamed. The teachers expressed their appreciation for having their voices heard, while the principal believed the teachers finally recognized her struggle to win their cooperation in implementing district directives.

As the parties gained insight into their own defensive styles, they came to appreciate the resistance that prevented contact. This awareness of varying perspectives and unmet needs opened the door to new ways of relating. The weeks following that meeting were the calmest and most productive anyone could remember.

Resistance happens. It can occur in any system, at any level, at any time. How we respond either reinforces the resistance or allows us to work through it. When I urged Lynda to interact differently with the faculty, I believed that approach would help; in fact, my attempt to overpower the group's resistance caused them to become more entrenched in their positions.

Of important note in this example is the way a push in one direction brought a shove back. Lynda ignored the teachers because she was upset; the teachers demonstrated their displeasure by breaking rules. The forces within a system seek balance. This applies to intimate systems such as classrooms and larger systems such as schools. As leaders, we make changes intended to benefit one level of the system, only to find that we have created a problem elsewhere. We push for compliance, only to fortify resistance.

Leadership requires balancing the forces for sameness and change. We must provide a safe environment for risk-taking while we promote energy and excitement for change. This complex challenge requires a real appreciation for the intricacies of how systems stay in balance. A willingness to explore your own actions, whether helpful or harmful, provides important modeling for others within the system.

In this chapter we will explore several aspects of school culture that can be influenced by the ways we manage resistance. We present each aspect as a continuum, recognizing that the unique constellation of conditions within any school may place it anywhere along the continuum, but also mindful that the choices we make as school leaders can move us and our schools toward one extreme or the other.

Fragmentation to Cohesion

Gail, the principal at a suburban middle school, announces at a February faculty meeting that because student behavior problems during the lunch break have escalated, each department must supervise the cafeteria one day a week. She hands out schedules outlining the days and periods. Almost immediately, the social studies teachers begin to grumble; their assigned time in the cafeteria conflicts with a weekly informal gathering their department established last year. They point out this conflict, but before Gail can respond, the math teachers speak up; the schedule works for them—in fact, they can't switch to any other time. Other teachers start to chime in. Tapping her pencil briskly on the table, Gail stops the discussion and tells the social studies teachers, "None of the other departments have a problem with the schedule—we can't tinker with it now."

Gail has overpowered the resistance from the social studies teachers, but the way she did it—in effect, setting one department against the others—triggers an unintended chain of events. The social studies teachers nurse their resentment. Minor squabbles break out between them and teachers in other departments. As tensions rise, department heads grow territorial about classroom supplies and audiovisual aids they once shared. An argument even erupts about who is responsible for replenishing the coffee filters in the teachers' lounge. The resulting fragmentation eventually takes its toll on many facets of school culture, including decision-making, team building, and certainly job satisfaction.

Fragmentation isn't always this intense, but it is quite common and always destructive to school culture. In the extreme, fragmentation can hinder trust, communication, teamwork, and overall productivity. All of these consequences reduce efficiency and may invite the implementation of new policies and procedures that almost certainly reduce the autonomy of teachers and students.

As leaders, we must work through resistance without creating the tiny fissures that lead to larger cracks in our school communities. When we explore resistance with curiosity and respect, we bring people together to solve problems in ways that unite rather than divide. In this scenario, for instance, Gail might have allowed the departments to work together to design the schedule—or at least recognized the inconvenience to the social studies team. Their resistance might have dissipated, and the satisfaction of problem solving would have brought the faculty together.

Dissension to Commitment

Ms. Carroll promises her fifth grade students that she will allow them to listen to music during the last few classes before summer vacation—*if* they all earn a B or higher on the final exam. Eagerly, the students rally to meet this challenge. They encourage each other to study hard, help each other with tough concepts, and take advantage of every opportunity to prepare for the exam. All but two students earn at least a B. Because the whole class worked so hard—and because she doesn't want to make scapegoats of the two who fell short of the goal—Ms. Carroll decides to grant the reward.

The following day, she brings a radio to class. Several students rush to tune in a station. After some jostling, they settle on a station playing a song that many of the students obviously recognize. As they begin to sing along, tapping feet on the floor and pencils on desks, Ms. Carroll starts to make out some of the words—abusive language and lyrics demeaning to women.

Scowling, she marches over to the radio and shuts it off. "How can you listen to such garbage?" she asks. The students are first confused, then outraged. A heated debate ensues. Ms. Carroll argues for civility and respect, while the students defend free speech and artistic license. "They don't mean what they are saying," they insist. "Just because we listen doesn't mean that we believe it."

The students' arguments don't convince Ms. Carroll; in fact, they seem to stiffen her stance. She disparages their music and dismisses their ideas as naïve. In the end, she makes them change the station to one that meets her approval. When they continue to gripe, she threatens to take the radio home for the rest of the week. Finally, they give up. The next day, the classroom routine resumes—with elevator music playing in the background.

Instead of improving the classroom atmosphere, Ms. Carroll's response has soured it. Instead of rewarding and reinforcing her students' commitment to learning, she has lost their respect—not because of how she felt about their music, but because of how she treated their resistance. The last week of school saw the students disengage emotionally. A similar event earlier in the school year might well have led them to test other limits.

Such dissension erodes the fabric of a school community. It widens the distance between leaders and followers, diminishes respect for rules, and engenders dissatisfaction and tension.

If Ms. Carroll had worked through her students' resistance less impulsively, exploring their beliefs and attitudes, they might have responded in kind. Instead, she lost an opportunity to model empathy, dialogue, and healthy communication.

As leaders, we have the responsibility to model this approach. We set the tone for how problems are resolved. If we ride roughshod over resistance, we create an environment where toughness prevails. If we shrink from conflict and allow others to get their way, we foster an atmosphere of cliques and distrust. But if we respect others, empathize with their views, and work with resistance, we strengthen our community's commitment to each other and to the objectives we share.

Inefficiency to Productivity

As principal of a struggling school, Connie urgently needs to improve faculty morale. She works with Jim, the district superintendent, to develop a three-part incentive package: (1) time off, at the principal's discretion and with in-school substitute coverage, for teachers who put in extra hours; (2) recognition for teachers who consistently exceeded expectations, in the form of small gifts purchased with professional development funds; and (3) a new evaluation program based on teacher strengths rather than performance critiques. Each proposal involves policy changes that the school board must approve.

Jim wholeheartedly supports the program, but the school board balks. At three successive meetings, the proposals are tabled. The superintendent blames the delay on "personality conflicts." Shortly after his appointment as superintendent a year ago, he had rattled the board with strong statements about their priorities. As a result, several board members take a dim view of any initiatives Jim proposes. Unfortunately, this resistance has the effect of blocking progress at each of the district's seven schools.

In Chapter 5, we observed the same dynamics at work in a smaller setting, as Mrs. Overton dismissed Jeff's protests at a surprise test. By overpowering her students' resistance, she gained her objective of completing the chapter test, but their performance suffered.

People don't work efficiently when conflict distracts their attention; organizations and systems don't function efficiently when friction draws off their energy. Unless we harness the forces of resistance, they will distract us from our goals. As leaders, we must manage resistance in ways that enhance productivity.

Solitariness to Teamwork

It's near the end of December at a suburban school in South Jersey. Betty, a special education teacher, has closed out her Individual Education Plans as required by school policy. But the next morning, she walks into her room to find a stack of individual education plan (IEP) forms for next semester's class on her desk. Nobody has warned her that this work was coming; there's not even a note. Resentfully, she starts to fill out the forms.

Across the hall, Jack rummages through his desk looking for a whiteboard marker that actually has some ink left. Betty can hear him grumbling; every time he replenishes his supplies, the art teacher walks off with the new markers.

Meanwhile, a gym teacher storms into the main office. "Why didn't anyone tell me the maintenance department planned to refinish the gym floor this week? I scheduled a volleyball tournament for Wednesday night!"

Up and down the corridors, teachers harbor their separate grudges and pursue their separate goals. Nobody takes responsibility for moving forward; each blames someone else when problems arise. A survivalist mentality prevails.

One teacher offered a vivid image of the way individuals protect their own space within an organization, calling it the "egg carton syndrome." Each person draws boundaries that circumscribe a limited safety zone. Within their separate shelters, people seek to meet their own needs and achieve their own objectives. They limit contact with their colleagues to the bare minimum. Teachers don't volunteer to cover each other's classes; people don't share information or other valuable resources; the administration makes decisions without consulting those affected.

This atmosphere of isolation and antagonism develops when school leaders view resistance as a threat and respond by overpowering, circumventing, or avoiding its force. By contrast, leaders who manage resistance in healthy ways—with curiosity, empathy, and awareness—engender a shared ownership of the process and outcome. When leaders and subordinates share responsibility for goals, they have a better chance of reaching them. Even more importantly, as people work together toward common objectives, they join forces as a team that is stronger than the sum of its individual members.

The way we manage resistance affects every imaginable aspect of school culture: communication, decision making, policies, and procedures, and ultimately job satisfaction. As teachers respond to resistance among themselves and with their students, they shape the learning environment and model problem solving, conflict resolution, and adaptation to change.

Armed with the knowledge you have gained thus far, you can take steps to move your school farther along the continuum toward healthy adaptation to change. Take a good look at your school community. Identify an aspect of the school or classroom culture that needs attention. Explore how new ways of managing resistance might make a difference.

Summary

♦ The way we manage resistance determines whether people come together to solve problems or split into quarrelsome factions.

♦ When we demonstrate respect for differences, we strengthen our community's commitment to shared objectives.

♦ When we harness the forces of resistance, we make its energy available for productive work.

♦ Where solitary operations prevail over collaboration, people may feel safer but often less satisfied.

Suggested Reading

Bates, C. (2001). *Pigs eat wolves: Going into partnership with your dark side.* St. Paul, MN: Yes International Publishers.

Part IV

Putting Change into Practice

9

The
Nature of Change

Change—even a change as simple as accepting a new concept, acknowledging a feeling, or altering a behavior—implies movement, and movement requires energy. Change within schools involves adjustments at three levels: the intrapersonal level (within the individual), the interpersonal level (between individuals), and the group level (faculty, school, district, and various subgroups). Leaders must consider the complex interplay of all these levels as they navigate change.

At each level, people invest energy either to support the change or to maintain sameness. If the momentum of energy favors change, that outcome will win through; if not, the forces for sameness will prevail. Energy is gained and lost through excitement and fear, through resistance and our responses to resistance.

In this chapter, we explore the nature of change. The more we understand the process of change, the better we can predict the various stages at which resistance can take place—and the better we can map out our response.

The Cycle of Change

Change is best understood as cyclical; every ending brings another beginning, and every beginning opens an indefinite number of possibilities about the outcome. Each person within this loop of possibility influences its course. Some work to propel the change along its current path; others attempt to redirect its course; still others try to slow it down or bring it to a halt.

Within this cycle, every change starts with an idea or concept, framed as a belief or triggered by experience. We consider the information and assimilate its implications, either internally or in a discussion with others. After identifying our options, we choose a course of action and mobilize energy to make some choice of action in order to carry the desired goal.

Figure 9.1. The Cycle of Change

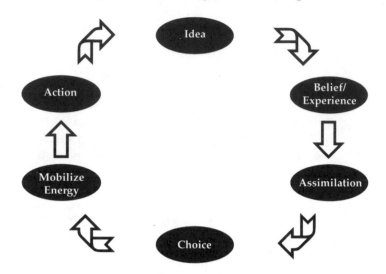

For example, a school might want to address the issue of summer reading. Experience shows that teachers aren't following through in the fall. The principal believes that providing an incentive to students would help solve the problem, so she proposes allowing students who read at least four of the books to spend their study hall hour in a comfortable area of the library instead of at their desks. (She considers establishing consequences for those who don't read, but decides against this.) Enlisting a group of teachers who support the plan, she works out the details and sends a memo home with the reading list in June. Come September, she will observe what happens and perhaps start a new cycle.

Approaches to Change

People and organizations take different approaches to change: reactive (taking action after the event), proactive (taking action before an anticipated event), and active (oriented toward the present).

In the reactive style, people wait for problems or issues to arise and then formulate a response. Reactive organizations hum along until change is needed, then intensify their energy. Reactivists may often function in crisis mode, which can strain the resources of the system. Until crises occur, however, the system largely stays calm—a strength of this style.

On the opposite end of the continuum is proactivity. Individuals or organizations that anticipate the need for change follow a more vigilant and vigorous cycle. Quicker paced and better prepared, they are able to conserve their resources in times of crisis. However, they may waste a certain amount of energy foreseeing the need for change, or take impulsive steps in unnecessary directions if they see a need for change where none exists.

The most balanced approach to change lies midway between the reactive and proactive style. Active people or organizations balance the conservation of resources with the application of preventive measures. Activists stay in the present while appreciating the lessons of the past and the possibilities of the future.

Most schools tend to approach change reactively. Faced with limited resources and an overwhelming amount of work, school leaders may not have the time or energy to anticipate problems; they have their hands full with today's concerns. Age and experience make a difference here; for instance, veteran teachers or administrators may lean more toward traditional approaches to teaching, managing behavior, and even organizational development. Change may come more slowly and painstakingly in schools where reactivity predominates. Leaders at such schools must appreciate the forces for sameness and manage them carefully as they seek to introduce more progressive ways.

Proactive schools—a minority—typically have less confident leaders and younger faculty. These schools may escape the survivalist mentality that keeps leaders focused on just making it through the day and the year. Instead, their leaders look apprehensively toward future problems.

Schools with an active approach to change tend to be highly adaptive. They value resistance and harness their constituents' energy to promote growth. These schools also recognize that not all change is the same; rather, there are three types of change.

Types of Change

Organizations can implement three different types of change: incremental change, transitional change, and transformational change. The type of change an organization favors reflects its style of adaptation—that is, the way it tends to respond to internal and external pressures.

Incremental Change

Incremental change—the most common form—occurs in segments. Those who choose incremental change tend to emphasize improving the parts, rather than paying attention to how the sum of the parts influences the whole. Incremental change involves low risk and low yield; it promises a fairly predictable outcome but offers less potential for significant growth.

Highly reactive schools tend to favor incremental change, constantly introducing new measures to counterbalance the effects of the ones that came before. They look at short-term consequences; as a result, they often need to implement upgrades to compensate for unforeseen effects. Rather than introducing new strategies, they focus on fine-tuning the strategies already in place.

One example of incremental change is the core knowledge movement (Hirsch, 1996), which reportedly helped more than 200 public schools in 37 states reform their elementary curriculums. Schools find incremental change appealing because of its specific, concrete design and implementation. The choices schools make for incremental change may not carry them toward a long-term goal or vision, but they make sense for the present moment.

Incremental change has its advantages—the ever-present hope of something better around the corner, the easy assurance that improvement is underway. On the other hand, a constant stream of incremental changes can prove burdensome to those who must implement them and disruptive to others. In particular, imposed changes trigger resistance, and changes promoted by outside specialists elicit skepticism. Whether it's the latest book on school reform or the popular speaker touting yet another concept for school improvement, it all looks very similar to experienced insiders who long for deeper and more permanent reform.

Transitional Change

Transitional change involves moving from one condition to another, generally facilitated by a new policy, new leadership, or a new challenge. Transitional change presents high risk and variable yield; its outcome is uncertain. The uncertainty and scope of transitional change may contribute to resistance; especially if people within the organization are comfortable with the present condition, the forces for sameness can exert a powerful pull.

Transitional change often requires a repositioning of elements within the organization. The resulting movement may jostle people out of their familiar positions into new relationships. Factions may form as alignments shift. Leaders can anticipate pockets of resistance—not only resistance to the change itself, but dissent among various factions.

For instance, when Michael Bloomberg was elected mayor of New York in 2002, he restructured the entire city school system. Teachers were told to lead from the side rather from in front; instead of delivering their lectures or opinions as experts, they were to provide direction as facilitators of learning. Spontaneity replaced prepared lesson plans; group interaction supplanted individual instruction. Along with this major shift in philosophy came a reshuffling of positions and duties. Special-education supervisors were eliminated, as were district offices. Teacher coaches and parent coordinators were added.

Resistance to the change rippled through multiple levels of constituents. Some faculty welcomed the new teacher coaches; others resented the intrusion into their classrooms. Parent coordinators were initially viewed with suspicion; where did their allegiance lie? The removal of special-education coordinators raised tensions between special-ed teachers and principals.

Transitional change can yield powerful improvements, but it also carries the risk of fragmentation. Leaders of schools that undertake transitional change must watch for realignments and guard against the possible loss of cohesion.

Transformational Change

Some organizations appreciate process more than outcome—that is, they pay more attention to *how* things get done than to *what* gets done. For instance, a school might raise its test scores a full five percentage points over the year but question the value of this outcome if bullying increases and teachers object to their reduced autonomy. Sometimes the end doesn't justify the means.

Such organizations are good candidates for transformational change—a high-risk, high-yield style of adaptation that focuses on *what already is* rather than on moving toward *what should be.* Schools that pay attention to the here and now often have an easier time working with resistance than schools that feel greater urgency about reaching future objectives and goals.

As a consultant, I often hear from schools that find themselves in distress because they have lost sight of what they had as they strove to become something different—a common pitfall for proactive schools. I don't discourage these schools from working toward their goals, but I do try to help them pay attention to how they navigate change.

Some changes that appear to be transformational may actually be incremental or transitional. For example, the philosophy of learner-centered schools (Darling-Hammond, 1997) offers a blueprint for transitional change—a paradigm shift with a clear end goal in mind.

Transformational change is not for every school; for one thing, it requires a tremendous commitment of resources. On the other hand, the very endeavor offers rich rewards. Those who lead their schools on such a course often appreciate the journey as much as the destination.

No matter which type of change a school chooses—incremental, transitional, or transformational—its leaders must evaluate the process carefully. Has the change brought the intended outcome? In particular, a school that finds itself introducing changes year after year would do well to stop and take a good look at the balance between content and process.

Summary

- Change follows a cycle. Beginning with an idea, it moves through belief and assimilation to choice, mobilization, and action.
- People and organizations may approach change proactively, actively, or reactively—anticipating issues, meeting them in the present, or responding after they arise.
- Incremental change moves an organization from one situation to another in small measured steps.
- Transitional change deliberately shifts an organization from one condition to another.
- Transformational change focuses more on the process than on the outcome.

Suggested Reading

Darling-Hammond, L. (1997). *The right to learn: A blueprint for creating schools that work*. San Francisco: Jossey-Bass.

Hirsch, E. D. Jr. (1996). *The schools we need: And why don't we have them*. New York: Random House.

10

Common Areas of
Resistance

Strong leaders promote an open environment of exchange and creativity, where people feel valued and respected. They encourage teamwork and self-discovery but also provide limits and reasonable expectations. Most of all, effective leaders approach resistance in a spirit of curiosity and adventure.

Every school has its hot spots—areas where resistance tends to crop up. In this chapter, we'll take a look at some of these hot spots. As you read, think of how you handle resistance in similar situations. If you can identify the strengths and limitations of your current approach, that awareness may pave the way for improvement.

Staff Meetings

In the early 1990s, I spent several years directing various organizations. At one program, my staff members enjoyed working with one another and were very invested in their jobs. Their efficiency and productivity made our work both enjoyable and rewarding. Our weekly staff meetings followed an established and consistent agenda; to an outsider, they would probably have seemed orderly and decisive. But while these meetings were productive and the staff members seemed content, I felt that something was missing.

Sometime during my tenure in this administrative role, I attended a week-long workshop on organizational consulting. The training evoked powerful questions about leadership styles, particularly how each of us worked through our own resistance. By the end of the workshop, I was prepared to undertake an experiment to change the nature of my program's staff meetings.

An experiment attempts to alter an experience cycle to yield new behavior. In my case, I planned to relinquish control, sacrifice some efficiency, and attend more to the *process* of the meeting (how we interacted) than to its *content* (the topics we addressed). My hypothesis was that focusing solely on content made people feel less important than tasks.

So I discarded the agenda for the staff meeting and opened the floor for staff members to address any topic that mattered to them. Naturally, I worried that the meeting would degenerate into a platform for complaints—and sure enough, complaints did surface. But the meeting soon took on a new tone. As I facilitated open and honest exchange—reflecting feelings, encouraging ownership of responsibility—staff members began their own problem solving. By the end of the meeting, they had resolved some longstanding issues and gained a deeper level of closeness.

Previously, I had thought that my proficient organization and structure made our weekly gatherings productive and efficient. This experiment taught me that by controlling the meeting so tightly, I was circumventing any resistance rather than exploring it. I learned that even a process that looks like smooth sailing can benefit from a subtle adjustment.

Evaluations and Observations

Perhaps the most stressful events in a teacher's year are the scheduled observations and assessments from supervisors. Does my lesson plan follow the curriculum as outlined? Will my students behave, or will they make me look incompetent? Will my nervousness show?

The Kansas City Chiefs, a professional football team, had a very disappointing year in 2002, winning just half their games. In 2003, they won their first eight games and seemed as though they were headed for the Super Bowl. What made the difference? The turnaround came after a confrontation between the coach, who had initiated harder workouts, and the players, who found this unfair. Instead of quashing the rebellion, the veteran coach listened and negotiated some compromises. The coach did this because he cared—cared so much that tears came to his eyes in a nationally televised interview as he described his connection to players five decades younger. (How many principals feel this way about their faculty?)

The NFL isn't a school system, of course. But principals, like coaches, face the challenge of managing resistance. If principals recognize that evaluations create stress and often engender resistance, they can give that energy some space to breathe. Allowing teachers to express their dissatisfaction with the way evaluations take place or their results may keep resistance from growing into outright opposition.

Keep in mind, too, that the typical evaluation system has its flaws. In this inherently subjective process, personality differences often come into play. Under the standardized curriculums often used nowadays, teachers must sometimes implement lesson plans that aren't altogether their own. A teacher's performance reflects strengths and weaknesses that lie along a continuum; someone with strengths in promoting organization and discipline may be less strong with flexibility and individuality. That teacher might receive a more favorable rating from a principal who values organization than from a principal who values flexibility.

One way to make evaluation more useful to teachers (and thereby reduce their resistance) might be to involve them in rating themselves. A teacher who views observations and evaluation as meaningful tools for professional growth may be more open to the process. Positive evaluations that express appreciation for past successes can motivate even veteran teachers to expand their horizons and upgrade their skills.

Staff Development

Many teachers view staff development as a waste of time. Instead of looking forward to in-service days as opportunities to stimulate professional growth, they dread them. Their resistance may take the form of apathy (they simply tune out), avoidance (they don't show up at all), or outright protest (they attend but complain bitterly). School leaders who detect such resistance would do well to explore it openly. No school can afford to waste its teachers' precious time and energy.

One New York school recently introduced an in-service exercise called "the final word." Each faculty member was to speak for two minutes about the topic of the day—in this case, the do's and don'ts of effective teaching. When one teacher raised a hand to ask a question, the principal shut her off: "This time isn't for discussion, it's for sharing." Though she listened patiently to all the "sharing," her question remained unanswered. Like many of her colleagues, she left the meeting feeling frustrated. Can you imagine that she would take this exercise back to her classroom and give her students "the final word"? And yet that was one stated purpose of this professional development session.

Professional growth and development is a component of organizational health; if done well, it can enhance the vitality of the school culture. Bluestein (2001) suggests that the quality of professional development opportunities correlates directly with the atmosphere of the entire school. Stimulating learning opportunities engender creativity and improve productivity.

Do the teachers in your school view staff development with apathy or hostility? As you read this book, consider how you might apply some of the ideas explored here to transform that resistance into creative energy.

Dealing with Parents

After the recent restructuring of the New York City schools, a parent coordinator on Staten Island found herself in an awkward position. A mother called to complain that her daughter felt intimidated by her teacher and was afraid to go to school. She asked the coordinator to have her child placed in a different class—but before hanging up, she also described a complicated array of issues on the home front, including an alcoholic husband who was returning home from a drug rehabilitation program.

The coordinator first approached the teacher, who refused to call and appease the parent. She then took the matter to the principal. Much to her surprise, the principal told her not to engage in prolonged conversations with parents, but to keep her calls as brief as possible.

What had happened here? Instead of embracing the parent as a partner and joining with her to address her daughter's concerns, the teacher and principal saw her as a threat in need of containment. Of course, schools have their hands full with what happens in the classroom; it's understandable that the teacher and principal hesitated to get involved with this parent's issues. On the other hand, the response of cutting short communication obviously failed to address the child's needs.

In fact, the interplay between parents and schools is a complicated dance. Parents expect schools to educate their children. If a child doesn't get good grades, the parents may hold the teachers responsible. In turn, schools expect parents to support their efforts. When schools view parents not as obstacles but as valuable resources, they open the door to useful alliances. But communicating with parents means more than talking with them for five minutes during parent-teacher conferences, more than sending home weekly notices, more than putting up a web page complete with lunch menus and lesson plans.

Do you remember the 1988 movie *Stand and Deliver*? An unemployed single mother kept her daughter out of school to help at home. The principal and teacher responded not just by trying to convince the mother to send her daughter to school, but also by helping her find work. If every teacher across the country did something like this for just one student, imagine how much parental resistance could be converted to support.

Dealing with Students

No list of hot spots for resistance in schools would be complete without mention of the liveliest group of people who enter the school building each day—the students themselves. Here we take a look at the potential areas of resistance in elementary and secondary schools.

In Elementary Schools

Elementary schools are playgrounds for experimenting with resistance. From the moment we are born, humans want to feel connected yet unique; we need to belong, and at the same time we need to be recognized for our individuality. This push and pull of opposing forces continues throughout each child's early years.

Teachers witness this developmental conflict firsthand. Kindergarten teachers can tell about parallel play, the need to have peers nearby but not actively involved. Third grade teachers observe young boys and girls teasing each other to express their feelings of affection or admiration. These preadolescents want to get close, but emotional or physical intimacy makes them uncomfortable. Fifth grade teachers see a constant rotation of friendships as their young charges experience the conflict between acceptance and rejection, fitting in and standing out.

In addition to these intrapersonal conflicts, classroom situations bring interpersonal conflicts. Teachers have expectations about student behavior, work ethics, and responsibility—expectations that may require growth on the part of their students. If the expectations reflect the teacher's personal agenda rather than the child's developmental needs, the child may experience a natural resistance. For example, a gregarious child who enjoys a stream of chatter with his classmates may well chafe at the rules if his teacher prefers quiet in the classroom. Given enough time, the student may begin to feel targeted, while the teacher perceives the student as oppositional.

Effective teachers seek a balance between nurturing each student's individuality and maintaining an orderly learning environment. Often, this means navigating their way among conflicts such as these.

In Secondary Schools

Middle and high schools incubate a more sophisticated type of resistance. Shaping their identities, teenagers resist authority in every form. They can express this resistance in the amount of homework they turn in, the grades they earn, their classroom behavior, and a host of other areas. We typically interpret noncompliance as disregard, disrespect, or indifference—yet much of the time it is, in fact, resistance.

If we understand this resistance in terms of the forces for change and persistence, then we can avoid unnecessary and harmful power struggles. If we try not to personalize resistance, we can help adolescents gain a deeper awareness of their own experience.

As adolescents push to test limits, they learn valuable lessons about life. As they develop the capacity for abstract thinking, they begin to formulate views about right and wrong. As they challenge established views and question society's structures, they are resisting sameness and pushing toward change.

Our task is to help them develop their social consciousness—but within the parameters of appropriate social behavior. For example, we may tolerate disobedience of certain rules, but not if this means harming a person or damaging property. Often, simply allowing adolescents a bit more space to experiment can lower their level of resistance.

Dealing with adolescents presents challenges, of course—especially when they display resistance, either as outright defiance or with more passive aggression. They know how to push our buttons, and they don't mind a power struggle; in fact, they relish it. As adults, we need to exercise control of the frustration, anger, and other strong emotions that arise when student behavior conflicts with our own need for power and control.

Suggested Reading

Bluestein, J. (2001). *Creating emotionally safe schools*. Deerfield Beach, FL: Health Communications.

11
Adaptation

Adapting to change is essential for survival.

Susan Osborn

We began this book by noting the tremendous challenges schools face. As we embarked on an exploration of how they meet these challenges, we chose to frame our evaluation not in terms of success and failure, but in terms of organizational health.

A school's organizational health depends on its infrastructure—its policies and procedures, its leadership, and the overall integrity of how it does what it sets out to do. It depends on the school's climate, especially the relationships among administrators, faculty, and students. Finally, and most crucially, a school's organizational health depends on its ability to adapt to change. Healthy organizations "not only survive in their environment but continue to cope more adequately over the long haul and continuously develop and extend their surviving and coping capabilities" (Hoy et al., 1990, p. 262).

Throughout this book, we have focused on how people in schools respond to change and deal with resistance. In particular, we have examined how school leaders can harness the forces of resistance to promote healthy adaptation. In this final chapter, we take a closer look at the ways organizations meet the changing demands of their internal and external environments through adaptation.

Adaptation Varies with Organizational Shape

Organizations rarely experience absolute agreement about movement toward change; every person or group within the organization responds to the initiative with some level of resistance (Janov, 1994). However, the size and shape of an organization makes a difference in the way it can harness the creative forces of that resistance.

A small school might manage a more supple response than a large institution; a school system that includes several facilities, each with its own focus and agenda, may develop more complex structures and procedures to manage change. Similarly, in an organization characterized by diversity, resistance may crop up for a wide variety of reasons and take a great many forms. In that case, adaptation will require a more intricate response, as well as more energy and more overall work.

As we have seen, resistance can lead to fragmentation. A larger system must work harder to remain integrated—that is, to keep its subsystems working in harmony rather than as adversaries. When the subsystems have different objectives and agendas, competition for resources may pose an additional challenge. On the other hand, a larger school or school system might have the advantage of greater resources.

Finally, each organization faces a unique and changing constellation of forces, both internal and external. Internal pressures range from union demands to management goals to faculty concerns; external pressures include parental attitudes, legislative changes, media pressure, and other community events. Any and all of these may affect the way an organization adapts.

Adaptation Depends on Awareness

A healthy organization practices self-awareness and then uses that awareness for positive growth. The Gestalt Institute of Cleveland (2002) has stated this premise:

> The reason one group or organization excels over another given equitable resources is the ability or competency of being able to scan one's internal and external environment, make meaning of the data collected and respond appropriately in ways that

support reaching agreed-upon desired outcomes (p. 14).

Healthy organizations also foster self-awareness among the individuals and subgroups within the organization. Janov (1994) uses the term self-regulation, recommending that "each individual and every organizational function understand their existences in relation to the system, and each self-regulate so that the entire system is enhanced" (p. 158).

In Chapter 6, we explored the paradoxical theory of change—the Gestalt concept that an organization must fully embrace *what is* before recognizing or pursuing *what may be*. For example, a violence-plagued school that implements immediate reactive measures—installing metal detectors, instituting peer mediation programs, or establishing a crisis response team—without fully exploring the roots of the problem may end up neglecting significant aspects of its organizational health.

Also in Chapter 6, we discussed the useful concept of polarities—the perspective that views reality as a continuum between extremes. An organization that practices self-awareness can identify its position along a relevant continuum, decide whether this position reflects where it wants to be, and choose to move toward one or another end of the continuum.

For example, a school struggling with teacher turnover may improve its recruiting efforts by thoughtful attention to its culture. Where does it lie along the continuum from structure to teacher autonomy? From a traditional to a progressive philosophy? The answers may help identify candidates who will thrive in the school's environment, or assist new teachers as they learn the ropes.

In particular, self-awareness helps organizations manage resistance and promote healthy adaptation. Throughout this book, we have seen how change disrupts equilibrium and resistance seeks to restore it. Healthy organizations pay attention to this experience of disruption and to the anxiety and excitement triggered by change. This awareness enables healthy organizations to foster excitement and reduce anxiety—in short, to harness the creative energy of resistance.

Adaptation Requires and Generates Learning

Schools are institutions of learning, of course. But learning is not reserved for the students. Healthy schools are *learning organizations*—living, growing entities that adapt purposefully to change.

Ikehara (1999) writes that learning happens in relation to an environment. In fact, learning may be a primary mechanism for how organizations adapt to their internal and external environments. DiBella and Nevis (1998) describe the learning organization as "having the capability to adapt to changes in its environment and to respond to lessons of experience by altering organizational behavior" (p. 6). Learning leads to adaptation—but because effective adaptation requires an appreciation of the results of change, adaptation also generates learning.

Product-based businesses experience direct and immediate feedback. The widget sells, or it doesn't; the factory runs efficiently, or it doesn't. Service industries monitor customer satisfaction; effective corporations rely on reciprocal feedback loops to ensure profitable growth. Schools cannot measure the impact of change so directly, but they must pay attention to its effects.

"The nature of learning and the way it takes place are determined in large measure by the culture of the organization" (DiBella, & Nevis, 1998). One important aspect of this culture is the organization's receptivity—or resistance—to new information. When organizations that foster a climate of openness and facilitate the free exchange of ideas, they promote healthy adaptation.

In Chapter 9, we saw how people and organizations take different approaches to change. Some react after the event; others focus on the present; still others take action before an anticipated event. The learning that accompanies adaptation will vary accordingly. For example, reactive organizations are more concerned with the past than the future. Poole (2001) states, "Organizations that anticipate change tend to be more successful because they develop knowledge, skills, and dispositions in advance of others" (p. 174). In her view, acting early expands the capacity to shape change. Finally, organizations that place a high value on learning will balance their anticipation of the future with recognizing the past.

In *How Organizations Learn*, DiBella and Nevis (1998) encourage organizations to explore their individual learning styles. Providing a useful framework for this endeavor, they describe seven learning orientations (ways knowledge is acquired, disseminated, and used) and ten facilitating factors (practices or conditions that promote learning). For each factor, they describe a continuum between two polarities. By identifying where it stands and where it would like to be along each continuum, an institution can increase its awareness of its own learning style. Armed with this awareness, the institution can adapt more purposefully to change.

Adaptation Reflects the Organization's Culture

Why do some schools adapt more effectively than others? One factor is the school's resiliency—its ability to respond to internal and external pressures while keeping a steady course. Highly resilient schools are likely to have a solid infrastructure and supportive climate that minimize the disruptive effects of change. Other aspects of organizational culture that promote healthy adaptation include professional growth and development, decision making, teamwork, supervision, and structure.

Professional growth and development in the form of stimulating learning opportunities enhances creativity and improves productivity throughout the school. Unfortunately, many school districts fall short here; teachers have little input, programs often lack quality, and cost-cutting measures usually target this area first.

Decision making—the process by which an institution formulates goals, makes plans, and resolves conflict—unquestionably influences the institutional climate. Effective decision making requires good communication at all stages and across all levels. The more—and the earlier—people have a say in a decision, the greater the likelihood that they will support it.

Teamwork and collegiality help build healthy, safe school communities (Bluestein, 2001). Constructive teamwork promotes mutual trust and support. By contrast, competition in the workplace may lead employees to feel guarded and isolated.

Supervision—the quality and quantity of oversight, direction, and support—establishes the tone in any workplace. Competent supervision fosters accountability and clarity; without it, workers may lack motivation and the school environment can fall into chaos. On the other hand, an excess of supervision can amount to intimidation, which discourages collaboration. "Intimidation is a great way to destroy community and back people into survival" (Bluestein, 2001, p. 356).

Last but not least, the *structure* of a workplace frames its culture. Loosely structured systems that yield uncertainty and constant change may have a very different climate than tightly controlled, highly organized systems. Susan Osborn (1997) presents a number of imaginative analogies—such as "white-water rafting," "motocross," and "king of the mountain"—to describe a continuum of structures, from rigid through chaotic, that contribute to an organization's culture.

Putting it All Together

Think of schools as giant incubators within larger laboratories. We experiment with cultivating the most effective product we can generate within the limitations of the tools and resources we are given. Just when it seems we have produced the right formula, the circumstances change and we are back to the drawing board. Similar to other scientists we try and approach setbacks with curiosity rather than disdain. We know that the question is not whether problems will arise but which ones and when; so the goal then is not to eliminate these problems but to learn from them.

How we approach this complicated maze of never ending challenges determines in large part the quality of the learning that takes place in the institution. As I have tried to convey throughout this book, the how is just as if not more important that the what. Just as learning can be used as a what, we must also examine the how in which it takes place, both for the students and for the faculty.

Working in schools requires patience and a high tolerance for ambiguity. The how is not always so easy to describe. We can oftentimes describe our experience in some fashion but words may not be so easy to find. The better job we do at listening to our experiences and scanning our environment however the easier it will become to describe what it is we perceive. A common language for articulating these shared experiences will pave the way for a healthier learning organization.

Remember that operating a school and running a classroom require constant readjustment to keep up with the changes of the environment in which they exist. Just when you believe you are close to achieving your desired outcome someone or something will always happen to disturb your plan. The forces for sameness and change exist for a reason, so remember that we are all part of something much bigger, the sum of which always exceeds the smaller parts we play.

Summary

+ Adaptation varies with organizational shape.
+ Adaptation depends on awareness.
+ Adaptation requires and generates learning.
+ Adaptation reflects the organization's culture. Factors include resiliency, professional growth and development, decision making, teamwork, supervision, and structure.

Suggested Reading

Banathy, B. H. (1992). *A systems view of education: Concepts and principles for effective practice.* Englewood Cliffs, NJ: Educational Technologies Publications.

Becoming a better interviewer. (1998). Organization and Systems Development Center (GIC).

Bluestein, J. (2001). *Creating emotionally safe schools*. Deerfield Beach, FL: Health Communications.

DiBella, A. J., & Nevis, E. G. (1998). *How organizations learn*. San Francisco: Jossey-Bass Publishers.

Hoy, W. K., Tarter, C. J., & Bliss, J. R. (1990). Organizational climate, school health, and effectiveness: A comparative analysis. *Educational Administration Quarterly, 26*(3), 260–279.

Ikehara, H. T. (1999). Implications of gestalt theory and practice for the learning organization. *The Learning Organization, 6*(2), 63–69.

Janov, J. (1994). *The inventive organization: Hope and daring at work*. San Francisco: Jossey-Bass Publishers.

Osborn, S. M. (1997). *The system made me do it: A life-changing approach to organizational politics*. Newark, CA: Life Thread Publications.

Poole, W. L. (2001). The teacher union's role in 1990s educational reform: An organizational evolution perspective. *Education Administration Quarterly, 37*(2), 173–196.